Organization of R&D: An Evaluation of Best Practices

Pradosh Nath
N. Mrinalini

First published 2002 by
PALGRAVE MACMILLAN
Houndmills, Basingstoke, Hampshire RC21 6XS and
175 Fifth Avenue, New York, N.Y. 10010
Companies and representatives throughout the world

PALGRAVE MACMILLAN is the global academic imprint of the Palgrave
Macmillan division of St. Martin's Press, LLC and of Palgrave Macmillan Ltd.
Macmillan® is a registered trademark in the United States, United Kingdom
and other countries. Palgrave is a registered trademark in the European
Union and other countries.

ISBN 0–333–99806–5 hardback

This book is printed on paper suitable for recycling and made from fully
managed and sustained forest sources.

A catalogue record for this book is available from the British Library.

Library of Congress Cataloging-in-Publication Data

Nath, Pradosh,
   Organisation of R&D : an evaluation of best practices / Pradosh Nath,
N. Mrinalini.

      p. cm.
   Includes bibliographical references and index.
   ISBN 0–333–99806–5
      1. Research, Industrial. I. Mrinalini, N., 1956– II. Title.

T175 .N28 2002
607'.2—dc21   2002070641

10   9   8   7   6   5   4   3   2   1
11   10   09   08   07   06   05   04   03   02

Printed and bound in Great Britain by
Antony Rowe Ltd, Chippenham and Eastbourne

To our parents

Contents

Preface

> At a time when many of man's organizations are faced with dissensions, stress, turnover, strikes, and conflict ... ... the organization that will remain viable, creative and relevant must engage in the process of search that the renewal effort involves.
>
> (G. L. Lippit)*

In today's fast changing world of technology, economics and politics, the question that may be asked is: How 'effective' are our Research and Technology Organizations (RTOs)? The answer to this question is especially crucial to the future survival of those RTOs operating in the not-for-profit or parastatal sector. For many of these organizations, both in the developed and developing countries, growing disillusionment with governments and the public in their effectiveness has led to calls for change in their purpose and organizational structures. That many of these organizations are currently facing the need for a new image has been a matter of intense discussion in several international forums and the subject of many studies since the early 1990s. The task of meeting this challenge has, unfortunately, not been given the same level of attention. For one thing, there has been a consistent lack of content in the many recommendations that have been made to address the situation. It is expected that this volume will begin to fill this gap.

The book addresses, in a concise manner, the underlying principles of 'knowledge' and 'knowledge management' which are at the core of the purpose and functions of today's RTOs. Most importantly, it examines the 'market' for the RTO and how this market may be identified and treated in the organizational structures of the RTO. The proliferation of management concepts and tools from the industry to the world of RTOs has led to a misunderstanding of what the 'products' and the 'market' of an RTO are. Should these be interpreted in the same way as in the industry? What are the conceptual difficulties in trying to equate 'knowledge' products with physical products from the industry? For the

---

* Gordon L. Lippit (1969) *Organization Renewal: Achieving Viability in a Changing World*, New York: Appleton-Century-Crofts.

manager of an RTO, the answers to these questions are vital if the changes to be introduced are to achieve the desired results.

There are several books and magazines on the subject of organizational theory and many more on management tools. But only a few of these are dedicated to the coalition of disparate organizations that we refer to as RTOs. The overall purpose of the RTOs is to bring the results of research, either created by themselves or by others, to application in industry, government or the communities they serve. This may be done through various means including consultancy and advice, training or the provision of management or technical services. As a general area of focus, RTOs tend to concentrate their efforts in helping and assisting small and medium enterprises (SMEs) in their attempts to innovate and grow.

This book is therefore intended to help managers of RTOs to initiate and manage the change process in their organizations towards achieving effectiveness. The lessons in the book will also prove useful to heads of research projects and programmes in these organizations. Furthermore, the book has practical ideas that can assist policy and decision makers in government and in international agencies whose duty it is to support these organizations – and often to evaluate and report on their performance and effectiveness. For students of research and technology management, the book presents an accumulation of the lessons learned from a cross-section of RTOs throughout the world, and also serves as a useful reference point.

The book draws upon the results of an international benchmarking project conducted by the World Association of Industrial and Technological Research Organizations (WAITRO) as well as similar studies from the authors' own RTO, the National Institute of Science Technology and Development Studies (NISTADS), India. It is the culmination of several years of research and teaching by two knowledgeable practitioners in the RTO environment. The authors have an impressive professional background in helping a variety of RTOs adjust to today's powerful pressures for change.

Moses Mengu
Deputy Secretary-General, WAITRO
http://www.waitro.org

Acknowledgements

This book is an outcome of an international project on, 'Strengthening Research and Technology Organizations' Capabilities to Support Small and Medium Enterprise Development', funded jointly by IDRC, Canada and DANIDA, Denmark, and coordinated by WAITRO, Denmark. We are very thankful to David Grier, Kristian Olesen, Niels Henrik Hansen and Moses Mengu for their valuable contribution during the project as part of the project team. We duly acknowledge the continuous support and active participation of Mr Ravi Maithel all through the project. Ashok Jain, ex-director, NISTADS, was encouraging and supportive all through the study. We acknowledge the continued support provided by Prof. Rajesh Kochhar, present Director, NISTADS. We thankfully acknowledge the valuable contribution of Mr S. N. Nandi, of the National Productivity Council, India, on benchmarking methodologies during the project work. We are grateful to the people of all the RTOs covered in the study, for their cooperation and support during our visits. Mr Rammi Kapoor of NISTADS helped us in literature survey during the study.

Abbreviations

ADG	Additional Director General
DANIDA	Danish Agency for Development Assistance
DDG	Deputy Director General
DSIR	Department of Scientific and Industrial Research
DTI	Danish Technological Institute
HOD	Head of Division
IDRC	International Development Research Centre
IRA	Institute of Research in Agriculture
IRT	Institute of Research in Textiles
JD	Joint Director
NCL	National Chemical Laboratory
NISTADS	National Institute of Science Technology and Development Studies
PI	Performance Indicator
PIU	Planning Information Unit
PS	Principal Scientist
R&D	Research and Development
RBC	Research Budget Committee
RC	Research Council
RTO	Research and Technology Organization
S&T	Science and Technology
SME	Small and Medium Enterprise
SRC	Saskatchewan Research Council
UNCTAD	United Nations Conference on Trade and Development
UNDP	United Nations Development Programme
UNIDO	United Nations Industrial Development Organization
WAITRO	World Association of Industrial and Technological Research Organizations

1
Introduction

The problem

It is a trying time for most of the non-corporate R&D organizations or Research and Technology Organizations (RTOs) as they are called throughout this book. Particularly those RTOs that are surviving on benevolent public funding are destined to witness a tougher time in future days of increasingly dwindling government support. Many of these RTOs have failed to foresee the changes in the role of the government from promoter of scientific and technological activities to the role of a major client of R&D output. The distinction between the roles of benevolent funders and judicious clients brings in the market dynamics to influence both public funding as well as the activities of RTOs. The government as a client would rely more on those RTOs that can deliver efficiently at the least cost and time. As a funder it would ask RTOs to be more market savvy and competitive with the rest of the world.

For RTOs, to be responsive to market means something more than just soliciting prospective clients. Does it mean RTOs operate like any other enterprise that produces and sells a product? Is there any distinction between a market savvy RTO and a successful business enterprise? Answers to these questions demand clarifications on the concept of RTOs. Such clarifications have to be based on an understanding of knowledge as a saleable commodity and market for knowledge, because RTOs deal with knowledge. Again, to be market savvy would also mean to tune RTOs' activities to the swings and moods of the market. Is the business of knowledge generation compatible with the market? Since the process of knowledge generation is different from the production process of any other marketable commodity, and since it is knowledge that is intrinsic in the superiority of a product or its production process,

1

knowledge-driven market is as much a reality as market-driven knowledge. The RTOs, therefore, have to position themselves in between these two types of drives.

Seen this way, the word 'client' (as users of RTO's knowledge output) gets a different meaning. Can the user (buyer) of knowledge be equated with a buyer of any consumer durables or non-durables? Is knowledge sold or can it be sold the same way as any other commodity? How is the intangible component of knowledge accounted for? Or, in other words, is the price of knowledge determined the same way as it is for other commodities? In the absence of an accepted price mechanism how do buyers and sellers come together? The case of RTOs, therefore, provides a new dimension of market where identities and roles of clients need to be redefined.

The successful repositioning of any RTO in an environment of knowledge competition and declining benevolence would be the result of its effectiveness in the generation and dissemination of knowledge. Is self-sustainability a necessary or sufficient condition for the effectiveness of an RTO? If it is the necessary condition can the dimension of knowledge generation be compromised for self-sustainability? If treated as sufficient condition, what would be the distinctive identity of an RTO? Or in other words what would be the boundary of RTO activities? Conditions of effectiveness of an RTO activity, therefore, have to be refined within the domain of knowledge-driven and market-driven activities.

Effectiveness depends as much on the choice of activity of an RTO as on organizational practices that conduct the activity. In fact, the choice of activity itself is a part of organizational practices that set the tune of organizational culture in an RTO. RTOs are organized efforts to induce the process of innovation within a given set of parameters defined by S&T and socio-economic systems. Such efforts are rather policy or strategy induced than market induced. By definition, therefore, market efficiency is subservient to organizational efficiency for inducing the courses of innovation in the system. Efficiency of an organization is confirmed by attainment of its goal. Again, demand on organizational efficiency varies in type and nature depending on the type and nature of expectations from the organization. Thus, RTOs in their earlier incarnation of assured public fund, and laid-back culture of generation and dissemination of knowledge had indulged in the kind of organizational efficiency that would be out of tune in the changing scenario where RTOs have to be more proactive in both accessing and disseminating knowledge. Organizational efficiency, therefore, cannot be left to be evaluated till the end of the attainment or non-attainment of organizational goals. On the contrary, organizational efficiency has to be effected so that the process of attainment of goals is controlled and monitored.

A functional definition of organization could be suggested in terms of a set of interlinked processes and practices. Organizational efficiency can be invoked by replacing bad practices by good or best practices. How do we identify good and bad practices? Is it possible to transplant one practice from a particular location to a different location? The question becomes important if we grant the culture and context specificity of a practice. This has immense implications for the restructuring of RTOs.

The framework

The questions raised in the previous section are some of the issues debated in this book. Most of the empirical inputs for the book have been drawn from a global study of organizational practices of RTOs. The World Association of Industrial Technology Research Organizations (WAITRO) launched the study with financial support from IDRC, Canada, and DANIDA, Denmark. The book deals with the question of restructuring RTOs in the new environment where they have to be competitive in the generation and dissemination of knowledge. The basic framework for dealing with the above issues is as follows. At the core of the argument is the definition of the effectiveness of RTOs. The definition formally enunciated in the book leads to the question of choice of RTO's activities between the two types of drives; knowledge-driven activity and market-driven activity. It is argued here that the dynamics of the growth of an RTO is the sustainable knowledge gap that it creates over the users of its knowledge-based services. Borrowing from contemporary literature, it has been argued here that RTOs have to create organization specific privileges. For doing so they have to choose knowledge intensive activities, where human resources and not the physical resource base will form the core. The knowledge base thus created will give a sustainable lead to RTOs over the users of its knowledge.

RTOs, therefore, are defined here not as revenue maximizing organizations but as organizations that maximize their knowledge base and in the process of dissemination they also earn revenue. This is how RTOs would be able to define their activities within the domain defined by knowledge-driven and market-driven activities. The effectiveness of RTOs, therefore, is defined by their ability to create and sustain the knowledge gap *vis-à-vis* the users, and also the ability to provide services capitalizing on the knowledge base that is continuously being upgraded.

What are the best organizational processes and practices that can make RTOs efficient enough to ensure the effectiveness defined above? This question has been tackled in this book by borrowing from the WAITRO study on RTO best practices. For the purpose of the problem addressed here, a few core organizational processes were chosen from the WAITRO study. The selected core processes together and independently influence the effectiveness of RTO activities. For choice of the best practice, it has been argued in the book, a distinction is to be made between the essence and logistics of the best practices. The essence is to be understood in terms of the basic principles whereas logistics would be specific to the organization adopting a best practice. Four basic principles have been developed based on contemporary understanding of organizational economics and organization studies, and practices under selected core processes individually analysed for identification of best practices. The analysis of best practices is followed by two cases of benchmarking study of organizational practices for methodological clarification and also for logistics of practices.

Adoption of global best practices is at the core of organizational restructuring for enhancing effectiveness of RTOs. But the organization that can effectively undertake such restructuring has to be a learning organization. An effort has been made to derive the implications of learning organizations for RTOs.

The structure of the book

In Chapter 1, we briefly discuss the evolution of industrial R&D as an organized effort under the patronage of the state. This chapter indicates how the role of the state or the promoters of RTOs changes over the years, and also the implications of such changes in the functioning of RTOs.

In Chapter 2, we briefly describe the WAITRO study in terms of its main focus, methodology and limitations. We have argued that in the new organizational dynamics the users are at the core. This implies that the achievements of an RTO need to be seen as its effectiveness *vis-à-vis* the users of its services.

In Chapter 3, we try to articulate the achievements of an industrial research organization in terms of its effectiveness. We suggest that such organizations are only as effective as their services. We also suggest that at the core of the effectiveness of industrial research are the human resources of an organization. In this chapter, we also try to identify the organizational attributes of the effectiveness of an RTO.

In Chapter 4, we use the WAITRO study of about 70 industrial research organizations to examine the types and nature of practices adopted by them for accessing and developing human resources. This chapter leads us to the question of best practices. Is it possible to identify organizational best practices for the human resource development of industrial research organizations? The WAITRO study adopted the benchmarking technique for this purpose. One of the major problems encountered in benchmarking exercises is regarding appropriate performance indicators for comparison among practices. Such problems are much more critical when we are dealing with organizational issues, because in many cases quantifiable indicators are not available, and sometimes not even desirable.

Chapter 5 discusses the issue in detail to defend qualitative indicators that have to be flexible and defined with reference to the practices. Such flexible and qualitative indicators have to satisfy certain generic principles of organizational dynamics.

Chapter 6 presents two exercises of benchmarking of RTOs carried out by the project team.

Chapter 7 relates the observation of an effective RTO with that of the characteristics of a learning organization. The last chapter is presented as a postscript. The postscript presents the concept of a vigilant organization that envelops the concept of a learning organization. It is argued that a successful benchmarking exercise can be undertaken by an RTO that is vigilant of the organizational form for enhancing organizational learning. The chapter makes a distinction between learning and vigilant organization. A vigilant organization can continuously learn and unlearn – the precondition for an effective benchmarking exercise.

2
A Brief History of Industrial R&D

State patronage of scientific research[1]

The present volume focuses on Research and Technology Organizations (RTO) engaged in industrial R&D and technology development outside the corporate sector. Corporate R&D or in-house R&D is a recent phenomenon. Earlier, scientific research organizations contributed in the form of inventions and innovations for industrial applications with the help of the state and private bodies.

The patronage of scientific research took different forms in Europe. In Germany, it was generally recognized that a close interaction between scientific institutions and industry helped production. Thus, there was liberal state patronage to universities and other scientific institutions.

This was not so in Britain. Till the first quarter of the twentieth century, science was patronized mainly by private organizations in Britain. However, at the beginning of the twentieth century, there was a growing realization that Britain was losing its industrial supremacy to Germany and the USA. The cause was thought to be a neglect of science and scientific research. This culminated in the establishment of the Department of Scientific and Industrial Research (DSIR) in 1916. It was felt that the DSIR would promote scientific research in collaboration with industry and other trade bodies for their benefit. Thus began a new era of state patronage of scientific research in Britain.

Around this time, big business groups in America were establishing cooperative research facilities. The involvement of industries was sought for promoting industrial research. It was suggested that autonomous research associations be used as an organizational mode. Instead of individual companies, whose resources were always inadequate for major scientific research projects, a group of companies or a whole branch of an industry would join together for a defined project and would cooperate with the DSIR on a pound-for-pound basis. A similar model was adopted in the then British colonies like India and Australia.

British scientific communities were euphoric over the assurance of government patronage to science. Although the contributions of British scientific institutions that were receiving government grants and other forms of patronage were commendable, the leadership of the British industry continued to decline. Thus, in 1964, the DSIR was disbanded and replaced by the Science Research Council. The same year saw the birth of the Ministry of Technology.

Scientific research to industrial R&D

The creation of a separate ministry for the promotion of technology was indicative of the growing realization of the complexity of the application of science in the industrial production system. It also highlighted the prominence of technology as an interface between science and industrial production.

Around the same time, economic research on technology-related issues led to two important findings. Solow (1957) estimated an overwhelming contribution of technology in the growth of the US economy. Arrow (1962a) argued that an environment of perfect competition could be conducive to minor innovations, but institutional intervention was necessary for major technological innovations.

After the emergence of the socialist world as a technological power, the rest of the world was convinced that technological capability could be earned, and that the path of technological progress could be planned. The well-directed launch of the Sputnik under the direct and strict control of the government was a case in point. A need was, therefore, felt for a technology policy that would ease the creation of R&D organizations under government initiatives and public investment in specific industrial and strategic technological interest.

Furthermore, while technology-related economic literature was rediscovering the contribution of technological strength to the growth of an economy, it was also understood that, left to market dynamics, firms would generally indulge in minor innovations. Direct institutional or non-market intervention was, therefore, considered necessary for major innovations that held the key to a global competitive advantage.

The result was the emergence of R&D institutions all over the world for technology development and technology-related services. Some European countries broadly followed either the German or the British model. The American experience was, however, different. It was the direct initiative and participation of large industrial houses that helped in technological advancement in America. With the end of the Second World War and the fall of Germany, it was the British model that became popular in the colonies and other aspiring new nations. Countries in Asia and Africa largely followed the British model. Many of the newly independent countries of Asia and Africa were closer to the socialist regime of the USSR. The British model of state patronage to scientific and technological research was in conformity with the broad socialist practice of state control of science and technology. Newly emerging nations, therefore, did not have much difficulty in adopting the British model, even though they were close to the Soviet regime.

The Second World War also saw the steady emergence of Japan as an economic power. The Japanese way of promoting science and technology was, however, different from that of the developed Western world. While the post-Second World War trend in industrialized countries was nationalization of industrial R&D or the public funding of R&D as formulated by Bush (1945), Japan and former West Germany followed the opposite policy of intensive involvement of private enterprises. In Japan, private sector industrial enterprises are responsible for most of the industrial R&D – presently constituting about 80 per cent of the total R&D expenditure of Japan. Government funding of R&D as a percentage of GNP from 1991 to 1993 was 1.07 per cent in the US (1993), 0.97 per cent in Germany (1991), 1.12 per cent in France (1992) and 0.75 per cent in the UK (1992) (Low *et al.* 1999). Compared to these figures, government funding has been 0.63 per cent of the GNP in Japan. It was with the Reagan administration that American policy firmly moved towards the privatization of industrial R&D (Slaughter 1993).

The sixties witnessed a significant rise in private funding of industrial research in Europe and North America. Contrarily, in Japan, government assistance to private industrial research showed an increasing trend as well as an increase in corporate research. Prior to the 1960s, it was the corporate sector that played the all-important role in industrial research (Nakayama *et al.* 1995).

In Japan, the government funding for R&D was generally used for funding the R&D activities of universities and national institutions where undertaking industrial R&D was against the post-war academic culture. Widespread student unrest in the 1960s in Japan was against what used to be construed as linking research with commercial interest. As a result, Japanese companies spent more on American universities than Japanese universities (Nakayama *et al.* 1995). Thus, the government funding of R&D being insignificant and universities being averse to commercial or industrial R&D, Japanese universities were relatively impoverished. Again, there were disparities between public universities and national institutions, with the latter taking away the lion's share of the government R&D budget. As a result, universities were left with hardly any resources for R&D activities.

Since the eighties, there has been a marked attitudinal change in university–industry cooperative research in Japan. In 1983, various Japanese universities and industries undertook 56 collaborative projects. The number increased to 396 in 1989. In the same year, the law that discouraged Japanese public universities from getting involved in profit-making private ventures was abolished.

Where should R&D be located – in universities, national institutions or corporate institutions? Should basic research (broadly known as university research) be completely isolated from applied research (broadly considered as a source of economically gainful R&D)? Are commercial R&D and non-commercial R&D two entirely mutually exclusive entities? Should R&D be directed only towards economic gains? The degree of emphasis varies from one country to another. Experiences with success and failure are also mixed. 'The dividing line between S&T, basic and applied research, and what one can deem as the most appropriate site of R&D, is a fuzzy one. While science tends to be equated with basic research and technology with applied research, both tend to justify themselves by potential economic spin-offs' (Ziman 1984).

Laboratory to industry: the great transition

It took quite some time to realize that the research results from the laboratory do not flow automatically into the production system. It also took time to discard the linear notion of innovation (from discovery to invention to commercial product) (Elzinga and Janison 1995). Some of the fundamental issues that cropped up were the science–technology interface, technology transfer from the laboratory to the production system and so on.

The reverse process is also now considered an important source of scientific research and discovery. There is now more clarity regarding the fact that developing a technology using the scientific results derived in the laboratory is far more resource-intensive (in terms of time, and physical and human resources) than the research itself. Again, research does not actually end in deriving results in the laboratory. And R&D is no less needed to make laboratory results work in real life. Engineering research is equally important to make technology work on the shop floor. Take the example of new superconductor materials. Although the principles of superconductivity were derived decades back, research is still on for developing a real-life superconductor with new materials. Research is being done, simultaneously, on the possible applications of the principles in various production systems. Such applications will finally need new engineering inputs with new superconductor material.

The problem, however, does not end here. The final application of any new technology depends on the preparedness of the production system. An in-house R&D system provides such preparedness. In Europe and the US, industrial houses have been investing in R&D and technology development since a long time. Industries are, to a great extent, geared to direct the course of R&D in state-promoted R&D organizations, and also absorb new research results from other R&D organizations.

Industries in the colonies and the new nations were in the nascent stage and in-house R&D capability was a far cry. Industrial culture was far behind the dynamics of technological competitiveness of Western industries. Therefore, R&D organizations following the British model encountered complex problems in giving direction to research and transfer of technology from laboratory to the production system. Thus, emulating an industrialized country in organizational arrangement for promotion of industrial R&D did not guarantee success in the developing countries. There were discrete successes of course. However, in general, industries would complain about half-baked technologies from laboratories. On the other hand, the laboratories would complain that industries were not interested in new innovations. There is truth in both the complaints. In the absence of an operating environment – industrial culture in this case – it is natural that the transplanted organization will not be as effective as it is intended to be. Over the years, therefore, there has been a growing concern about the efficacy of public investment in R&D organizations. This concern has two dimensions: questioning the performance of the laboratories in delivering or attending the technological needs of the industry; and questioning the sanctity of public investment for the benefit of the private industry.

From patron to client

The government has become one of the major clients of the services of R&D organizations. As a client, the government creates special funds for certain missions. For technology services and the development components of such missions, the government accesses the capabilities of R&D

organizations. Such missions are not restricted to government departments or ministries directly related to science and technology, but they could be from any ministry or department. As a result, R&D organizations now have a wider base of funds. However, such funds are tied to a specific purpose. They are not for the general development or sustenance of an R&D organization. Over the years, the availability of such government funds has grown in range and volume. The role of the government as a direct promoter of R&D organizations, therefore, has been gradually replaced by a more ubiquitous role through project-specific funding. In this mode, government projects and funds are not earmarked for any government-promoted organizations. They are accessible to any organization depending on its credibility. This has created opportunities for non-government R&D organizations. It has also created a competitive environment for government-promoted and -supported organizations.

State patronage under scrutiny

The result has been a gradual decline in state commitment for research laboratories created under state patronage. R&D–industry interaction has been found to be a general problem area. This interaction can possibly be induced by asking laboratories to generate resources from industries in the form of project funding.

The onset of globalization has, however, brought about a radical change in the scenario. In the context of developing countries, the market for their knowledge base is no longer restricted to an unresponsive domestic market. If they are worth their salt, they should be able to find a market for their knowledge base anywhere in the world. Amidst a few cases of success, a question has been raised about state patronage for benefits not restricted to domestic industrial initiatives. Going by the historical genesis of state patronage of industrial R&D, this question is relevant. State patronage had been sought, justified and granted for creating technological competitiveness in the domestic industry. Such arguments are not valid if institutions promoted by state patronage served the industrial interest beyond the domestic boundary. Thus, the justification for continuance of state patronage for industrial research took different forms. One line of argument is that technology or knowledge as a commodity has a wide international market. What the state, therefore, is expected to patronize is the promotion of knowledge-generation activities. The counter argument is that if knowledge is treated as a commodity and has a wide international market, then knowledge-generating organizations should be able to sustain themselves.

The other line of argument has been around small- and medium-scale enterprises (SMEs). In developed and developing countries alike, SMEs play a critical role in terms of the share of GDP and export. The role, however, differs according to the specific economic environment of a country. In the industrialized nations of Europe and also in the US, SMEs have an overwhelming superiority in high-technology areas (biotechnology and microelectronics) (Piore and Sabel 1984). In Japan, SMEs form the backbone of industrialization through links with large industries in a three-tier structure (two examples are the automotive industry and the synthetic fibre industry) (Itoh and Urata 1994; Furukawa *et al.* 1990). Lately, Korean industries have also started following a similar kind of structure (Kim *et al.* 1993; Kee *et al.* 1994). In developing countries, however, SMEs are seen as the best means of industrialization and entrepreneur development, particularly to address the perennial problems of capital shortage, unemployment and income-generation. In countries like India, the importance of the small-scale sector can be ascertained from the fact that this sector has been witnessing a higher rate of growth than the industrial sector as a whole. It contributes 40 per cent on an average to the gross turnover and 35 per cent to the total export of the manufacturing sector.

An interesting study by Rothwell *et al.* on the source of innovation brought out the fact that, unlike large enterprises, SMEs have a limited access to new technology and related services mainly because of their limited financial resources and market control. SMEs are, therefore, more dependent on external sources for technological support services. Large units, in many cases, either have an in-house system or have enough resources to access the desirable services from anywhere. SMEs, although eternally dependent on external resources, do not have adequate resources to access the desirable services (Rothwell 1990; Rothwell and Dodgson 1991). In the context of developing countries and in many industrialized countries, SMEs in many cases are not even aware of technological possibilities, potentialities and accessibility.

The importance of SMEs in the national economy and their dependence on external sources for technological inputs make a strong case for state patronage for technological services to SMEs (SRC 1988, 1992). Both in developed and developing countries, several government-level measures have been initiated to promote innovation in SMEs. These supports are mainly in terms of project funding, tax and other fiscal benefits, support for cooperative R&D, risk/venture capital support, and information and consultancy support. In most countries, these supports are extended to SMEs through organized networks of the government machinery and RTOs (Nanjundan 1986).

Challenges and responses

During the last fifteen years, most industrial research organizations have undergone a transformation along one of two lines: serving the client who can pay best; or serving domestic SMEs by accessing government programmes for a technology support system to SMEs. There are cases where RTOs follow a mixed path, serving SMEs and also selling technological knowledge to the best client. Irrespective of the nature of transformation, direct government patronage for industrial R&D can no longer be taken for granted. In many cases, the state has totally discontinued support to organizations that were being promoted by the state. In many other cases, state support has been substantially reduced. It has become more passive and R&D organizations have been asked to fend for themselves.

In the real life of an RTO, such a transformation means much more than just changing its client profile. It needs a total organizational revamping in terms of work culture, ethos, practices, accountability, and almost every dimension of the functions of an RTO. Araoz has noted the following problems associated with the organizational transformation of RTOs (Araoz 1996).

1. RTOs have failed to fulfill their original objective of assisting the technological development of industry. Many RTOs choose R&D activities of their own interest without focusing closely on the user industry and the changing technological needs of industrial enterprises. The result is a lack of success in the commercialization of R&D results.
2. In the present age of globalization, RTOs have to play the important role of assisting industries in enhancing competitiveness. Most RTOs are not geared to tune their activities with the competitive market situation.
3. RTOs need to update their capabilities and develop new skills. To keep pace with the fast-changing technological realities and resulting requirements of industries, RTOs have to update their human resources and capital equipment. In addition to human resource development in strategic areas, it requires a strategic alliance in various forms with other institutions – at home and abroad. Many RTOs, particularly in developing countries, lack long-term strategic planning of their future growth areas, capability-building and networking.
4. RTOs in the East European countries in particular are increasingly facing problems related to environment protection and adaptation of military technology for civilian use.

5. In many countries, the role of the state as a funder of R&D activities is declining. This has resulted in reduced resources for RTOs and a decline in their capability to serve industries at a time when they can be most useful. This, coupled with a general inertia on the part of the domestic industries, has raised the question of sustainability of many RTOs.

There seem to be two principal hosts of these problems.

One is resource-related. It began with declining state support. The RTOs suddenly found themselves in a situation where they were unable to take up new R&D projects and invest in human resource development. Thus, these RTOs became redundant to the industrial world where the technology scenario changes rapidly.

The other host is the work and cultural environment of RTOs. From the days of assured state patronage, RTOs were not tuned to a work culture where they were answerable to the users of their capabilities. In the new situation, be it for serving the client for revenue or for inculcating technological competitiveness among the domestic SMEs, RTOs have to be reoriented to become answerable to the users of their services. In the new environment, RTOs have to adjust their own areas of interest with those of the prospective or target users of their services. They have to continuously upgrade their human resources so that they can enter into new and emerging areas of science and technology and keep themselves ahead of the users of their services. And they have to do all these mainly with their own resources.

RTOs have to change their way of working. At the core of change, is the need to build up credibility with the users of their services. Credibility, therefore, has become the most important asset, albeit intangible, for the sustenance and growth of an organization engaged in research in industrial technology. It is not as if credibility was not important for such organizations in their earlier incarnations. Once established and created by the government, an organization would survive by the natural course of bureaucratic dynamics, where achievements are recognized but may not be the necessary condition for sustenance. On the contrary, in the new environment, an organization can survive only if it is an achiever or, in other words, its activities are effective for its clients. Organizations have to make concerted efforts to make achievements happen. It is to be noted that the core of the organizational dynamics is different in two cases, and so is the organizational edifice. What are the organizational practices that would create an organizational edifice of this new dynamics? As achievements have to be active pursuits in the new environment, R&D organizations have to be vigilant about organizational processes that enhance the scope of achievements.

3
The WAITRO Study on R&D Organizations

The importance of industrial R&D for technological capability-building cannot be overemphasized. At the same time, because of the various typical attributes of R&D activities, the performance of R&D organizations is subjected to regular scrutiny. One such attribute is uncertainty of return from investment in R&D over a real-time period. How can the best result be achieved from the investment made in R&D? The benchmarking exercise, therefore, has been initiated for the in-house R&D system of companies. Szakonyi (1994) has reviewed such an exercise for corporate R&D systems. Beyond corporate R&D systems, in most countries, governments have played an active role in creating a number of R&D organizations for the promotion of national science and technological capabilities. These organizations are either directly or indirectly funded by national governments. Most of these organizations are facing a tough time in terms of availability of funds and in justifying their effectiveness. Is it possible to revitalize these organizations through organizational restructuring?

The basic difference between corporate and non-corporate R&D is that in the case of the former, R&D activities are an integral part of the corporate strategy and goals. In the case of the latter, such a reference point is not available. Most of these R&D organizations have been set up to promote the creation of a knowledge base and its utilization in identified science and technology areas. As a category of non-corporate R&D, these organizations show various types of R&D orientation and ownership patterns.[2] Most of these organizations were initiated to augment investment in areas where private investment was not likely to flow naturally because of uncertain profitability. In developing countries where firm-level R&D was still at the nascent stage, R&D organizations were expected to play an important role in helping domestic industries to build up technological competence. However, they were located outside the production system, which necessitated and, therefore, needed an efficient organizational mechanism to forge a link with the prospective users of the knowledge to be generated. There are problems around such linkages in developing countries.[3] According to Bell (1993), the reason behind this alienation was that most of these institutions were set up following the European experience, much before the industries in developing countries achieved comparable status. Rush *et al.* (1995), however, argued that such problems were not uncommon in developed countries as well.

Quite a few studies have been conducted to evaluate technology research systems in different countries. Araoz's study on 'Revitalization of Technology Research Institutes in Developing Countries' gives a list and includes many such studies done under the auspices of UNDP/UNIDO/UNCTAD/IDRC. Most of the case studies included by Araoz and also those done by him deal more with the types of problems and less on how to solve these problems. Nevertheless, these studies initiated a debate on the organizational restructuring of R&D organizations. Araoz completed another study in 1999 on 'Best Practices among Scientific Research Institutes Responding to Strategic Challenges'. Rush *et al.* (1995) studied the application of the benchmarking method in research and technology institutes. The question, however, remains regarding suitable organizational structures and practices that can allay the problem of alienation between RTOs and the users of their knowledge?

In June 1994, the International Development Research Centre (IDRC), Canada, launched a project titled 'Benchmarking the Best Practices of Research and Technology Organizations (RTOs) for Strengthening the Capabilities of Small and Medium Enterprises (SMEs)' in collaboration with DANIDA, Denmark. The project was coordinated by WAITRO and carried out by an international team consisting of researchers from the Danish Technological Institute (DTI), Denmark; the Saskatchewan Research Council (SRC), Canada; and the National Institute of Science Technology and Development Studies (NISTADS), India.

The project was aimed at identifying a set of organizational best practices for making RTOs more responsive to their clients, particularly to their SME clients. The problem obviously has many dimensions. The social, cultural, and political specificity of the problem can never be undermined. The project, however, tried to examine the issue from the point of view of the management of the RTO as an organization meant for providing technological services to its target clientele. The approach stressed on having a target client, and building up a long-term relationship with the client on trust. The RTO's task, therefore, is not as an agent interested in selling off-the-shelf projects to enterprises, but making clients aware of the virtues of innovation and the new horizons of technology – the very *raison d'être* of the RTOs. What would constitute best practices for the envisaged role of an RTO?

Benchmarking RTO best practices

The methodology adopted for developing best practices is known as 'benchmarking' in business management parlance (Camp 1989; Boxwell 1994; Sprow 1993, 1994). Benchmarking has already outgrown its traditional field of applications like industrial engineering. By the late eighties, it became popular as a tool for executing corporate strategic planning. In the nineties, it became an integral part of the Total Quality Management programme. Now, a more precise articulation of benchmarking is available. Bemowaski (1991) defined benchmarking as plain and simple learning from others by accessing an already existing pool of knowledge so that the collective learning and experience of others can be used by those who wish to improve their own organizations. Thus, benchmarking can be used by an organization with well-defined objectives and goals. This encouraged IDRC and DANIDA, and researchers in WAITRO, DTI, SRC, and NISTADS to try the benchmarking approach in R&D organizations.

Benchmarking is, essentially, learning from the best in the trade. Methodological complexity arises in identifying the best. It is also important to know what to learn and from whom to learn, and how to implement whatever is learnt from others in a different organizational environment. 'What to learn' requires a clearly defined problem and a long-term strategy on the part of an organization. 'From whom to learn' requires identification of the best in the trade. If every aspect of an organization is to be benchmarked, it may be necessary to learn from more than one in various trades. Trades can be comparable and not necessarily the same as the trade of the organization to be benchmarked. It is more important that there is generic similarity of the activity to be benchmarked (Nandi 1995). Thus, an RTO can probably learn more from the hotel industry or retailing businesses in the area of client interaction and building up credibility with clients.

In the WAITRO project, however, a modified benchmarking technique was adopted (Nath and Mrinalini 1995). Three critical tasks were necessary for beginning the benchmarking exercise.

1. Dissect the core activity of a typical RTO. In benchmarking terminology this is called *process-making*.
2. Choose the *benchmarking partner*.
3. Develop a set of *performance indicators* for a comparative study of practices.

Process-making

This is basically dissecting an organization into core activities. Processes can be further divided into sub-processes. Sub-processes are micro-level actions or points of decision making. How detailed the divisions of sub-processes should be again depends on the overall objectives of the benchmarking exercise. At the same time, too much detailing could be self-defeating because we may drift away from the problem we want to address. A process is a set of practices that are functionally related to each other. If we break down processes into further sub-processes and sub-sub-processes we shall be left with processes with a single practice and miss out on the functionality aspects of practices that make a process active.

In the WAITRO exercise, ten core processes were identified for a typical RTO: the governance of an RTO, financial management, RTO services, business development, project management, capability-building, personnel management, networking, and policy and programme accessed by the RTOs.[4] These processes have been considered as generic and common for all the RTOs. Every process, thereafter, has been broken down into several sub-processes. For example, RTO governance (a process) has 10 sub-processes covering ownership, legal structure, governing body, mandate, mission and so on. A total of 57 sub-processes have been identified for 10 major processes.

Such divisions of organizational actions are not sacrosanct and entirely depend upon the perception of the benchmarking team as to the problem they are going to address. The division of an organization into processes and sub-processes is specific to a particular purpose (Singh and Evans 1993). An example from the WAITRO exercise will clarify the argument. Sub-processes like project selection and knowledge delivery system are treated in the WAITRO study as part of the process called project management, and human resource development is treated as a part of the process called capability-building. The same sub-processes, however, have been taken as independent processes in a benchmarking study that focused only on industry–R&D linkages (Nath and Mrinalini 2000).

Along with the specific purpose of the benchmarking exercise, it is important to clearly understand the mandate of the organization and the organizational structure. The core structure of an RTO envisaged in the WAITRO study is shown in Figure 3.1.

Clearly, in an RTO's organizational structure, the emphasis is on the RTO's capability-building which is considered as the backbone of its credibility to its clients. Araoz argued that one of the major problems for publicly funded RTOs was capability-building in isolation. In Figure 3.1, the activities of undertaking research and service arise out of close liaison with their industrial clients. Similarly, capability-building is also based on such liaison. Undertaking research activities itself is shown as a part of the process of capability-building. The figure provides the basis for an organizational architecture of an RTO. This understanding is critical for process-making (see Nath and Mrinalini 1996).

Choice of benchmarking partner

Once the processes and sub-processes have been identified, the next task is to identify practices and compare and measure them with the benchmarking partner. The easiest way is to choose the best in the business. Rush *et al.* (1995) have adopted this method for their study. But who is the best may be highly debatable. Given the socio-cultural and political specificity of RTOs in different parts of the world, it was not possible to identify, a priori, any one RTO as the 'best RTO' or any practice of an RTO as the best practice. Since the objective was to identify global best practices, it was realized at the outset that the 'best' practices would have to be identified among the population of the RTOs studied by the project. The WAITRO approach was to identify the best among many. In fact, in the WAITRO study it was realized at the very beginning that there may not be one best organization, and that one

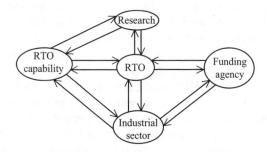

Figure 3.1 The core structure of an RTO

set of best practices for different processes may be found in more than one RTO. In the WAITRO study, therefore, there was no single partner. Again, from the methodological point of view, it was decided that it was not the best RTO that needs to be identified. Instead, it was thought to be quite possible that one RTO might not be the best in every activity. The task, therefore, was to compare all the RTOs with each other to determine a set of best practices among them. As a result, instead of benchmarking with one RTO, the benchmarking task was made more elaborate for comparing each practice for every RTO.

About 60 RTOs from all over the world became willing subjects for the exercise. Care was taken to include a suitable representation from both developed and developing countries. The exercise, therefore, can be called cooperative benchmarking. A major limitation of this approach is that the best practice can still be somewhere outside the selected 60 RTOs. Since the purpose of the WAITRO study was the refinement of the benchmarking methodology for the RTOs and also to create a reference point of best practices, the said limitation in choosing partners was ignored.

Performance indicators (PI) for selection of best practices

The choice of a benchmarking partner has implications on the methods of selecting the best practice. When the best organization is known, the RTO can replace, wherever possible, its existing practices with the practices of the best organization. If benchmarking is defined as learning from others, this will be copying and not learning; and practices cannot be replicated if they are not learnt. Learning, in this case, will need a generalized understanding of practices in terms of organizational principles. Every activity of an RTO and the supporting organizational arrangements have to be such that they directly contribute to the process of trust and confidence-building of the industries. This final criterion indicates the performance level for the purpose of identification of best practices. The project did not begin with any a priori idea of a best RTO and its practices being best practices. Instead, every important practice of an RTO was examined in terms of a set of performance indicators and RTOs were ranked for every practice.

In the case of the WAITRO study, the aim was to obtain a set of practices sub-process-wise from all the 60 RTOs. These practices were to be compared and best practices identified. This needed a set of performance indicators (PIs) for each sub-process. An effort was made to develop quantifiable indicators as far as possible along with qualitative indicators. Indicator sets were created using the overall financial performance of the RTO, the time and cost aspects of the practices, and also a qualitative assessment of the practices by stakeholders of RTOs and experts in RTO management. Since relevant information was not available for all practices of all the RTOs, a fully developed set of indicators could not be arrived at.

It appears that a rigid quantifiable set of indicators may not even be desirable. Practice means action that will have an outcome. The performance of an action is easy to measure if the outcome is quantifiable or, in benchmarking terminology, metrics are available. It should be remembered here that precise quantified data is not the essence of benchmarking. In fact, the benchmarking exercise must rely on imperfect data or actionable accuracy rather than totally factual and precise data. According to Sprow (1993), we benchmark the most important, and not necessarily the easiest to measure.

We, therefore, have to invent ways of comparing practices that are accurate enough to suggest actions. In the following section, with the selected process for RTO–industry interaction we shall illustrate some such actionable accuracy in comparing practices.

Table 3.1 is an example of the 'Governance of RTO' as a process. The table has taken the example of 'Ownership' of an RTO and shows the practices in that regard for all the 60 RTOs covered by the study. The practices thus identified have been compared with respect to a certain yardstick for best and good practices. For example, in the case of ownership, the question asked was which ownership type was the best for making an RTO most responsive to industrial needs. The practices, in this regard, have to be compared with respect to a set of PIs.

An effort has been made for developing a set of PIs for each subprocess. This was the most important, debatable, and difficult part of the whole exercise. Although a set of quantifiable PIs would have best served the purpose, unfortunately, except for financial information and information on staff strength in various categories, other types of information required for PIs was found to be qualitative in nature. Again, financial information, broadly speaking, is not quite useful as a direct PI of the non-profitable activities of an RTO. As such, if an RTO is created and run for making profit, it would not close business as long as the owner thinks that it is profitable. In such cases, the financial parameters would have to serve as a PI. However, most RTOs are not created as profitable business propositions. The RTOs, especially in cases of government ownership, are created with the broad national objective of technology-capability-building in specific areas. The government understands that the profitability of such ventures is sufficiently ambiguous for private

Table 3.1 Process: Governance of RTO sub-process – ownership of RTO

Practices	No. of RTOs in					
	Latin America	North Asia	Africa	Europe	Developing countries of Asia	Developed countries in Asia
Fully owned by national governments	6		13	1	11	1
Fully owned by prefecture, province, state, etc. government	1	3				6
Fully owned by industry associations				3	1	
Not for profit foundation	2	4		2	1	
For profit, privately owned						
Several national governments	1					
Several provincial governments		1				
University		2				

enterprises. Also, there is a strong feeling that if profit-making is the only aim, the goal of technological-capability-building may not be achieved. Again, in the case of developing countries, where industrialization and entrepreneurship are at the nascent stage, RTOs have to play a key role more in creating a market for their services and capabilities than simply responding to market needs.

These arguments indicate that simple financial performances of the RTOs cannot be correct indicators of best ownership types. Of course, if the owner of an RTO perceives its activity to be satisfactory, the RTO should not suffer from financial constraints. But, a 'no resource constraint' would only be an indirect indicator of the *raison d'être* of an RTO. In the study, therefore, quantifiable financial indicators have been complemented with qualitative information, like the RTO management's perception about ownership.

In fact, throughout the study, a set of PIs consisting of quantitative and qualitative information was developed. The quantitative information was mainly based on (i) financial performance, (ii) growth in the RTO budget, (iii) average revenue from clients, (iv) growth in staff, (v) growth in supporting staff, and (vi) growth in number of clients. This information was used for developing a set of indicators.

The qualitative information used by the study was the (i) management's perception, (ii) staff's perception, (iii) client's perception, and (iv) owner's perception.

A lot of this information was not available for all the RTOs and, therefore, could not be used to compare practices across the RTOs. But this information was considered most important for developing a set of ideal PIs. A set of ideal PIs would constitute those indicators that would allow a comprehensive comparison of practices over the RTOs.

These ideal PIs were, however, used to develop an ideal management information system (MIS) of an RTO with the understanding that such an MIS would help the RTO to continuously monitor and benchmark its practices.

The PIs were further supplemented by expert opinions on the best practices, sub-process-wise. In cases where there was inadequate information to develop PIs a set of experts was chosen on the basis of their experience and success in the governance of RTOs. Their opinions were matched with the results obtained from available PIs to arrive at a final choice of best practices.

Limitations of the study

The main limitation of the study was its population base. A constraint of time and resources prevented careful choice of the population base to suit the purpose of the study. The possibility, therefore, remains that many important practices would not have been accounted for. We have tried to overcome this problem by re-stating the aim of the study. Instead of looking for global best practices for the RTOs, we decided to look for appropriate methods of organizational benchmarking. While doing so, we also ensured that such an exercise was actually feasible. Again, the study could successfully identify variations in practices in a sub-process. It lent credibility to the best practices suggested by the study, and would be used as a reference best practice by the RTOs.

Next, there were methodological limitations in developing PIs sub-process-wise. The indicators based on qualitative information, like an assessment of the management or the staff regarding a particular practice could be gathered through limited interactions during the visit of the project team. Gathering information on clients' assessment of a particular practice was not easy. Many RTOs had a practice of collecting feedback from the clients. In some cases, such information was made available to the research team. In a few cases, the RTOs arranged meetings with clients during the visit of the project team. This information, not being available for all the 60 RTOs, could not be used for a general comparison of practices. However, it definitely provided an indirect insight into the comparative analysis of various practices. Take the case of the prefecture laboratories of Japan. A few laboratories gave us documented feedback of the clients on the practice of 'free on-site consultancy'. It was very difficult to quantitatively ascertain the merits of this practice. The clients' view, however, suggested that the main merit of such practices was that they helped to build mutual trust and one-to-one interactions with the personnel of RTOs and their clients. The project team learnt that more tangible transactions follow once mutual trust and dependence were established through appropriate practices. This lesson was useful in evaluating practices.

Another limitation was that the presentation of the balance sheets of the RTOs was so widely different that in many cases the financial returns were not directly comparable. The project team, therefore, had to use a mix of indicators to make practices comparable.

The WAITRO project was planned in two stages. The first stage was for developing a set of best practices. The second stage was for implementation of the benchmarking exercise for willing RTOs with reference to the best practices identified in the first stage. During the second stage, it was realized that many of the difficulties faced in the first phase were easy to overcome when dealing with the benchmarking of a single RTO. This was because it was easier to compare the practices of one RTO with a set of best practices than compare the practices of 60 RTOs. Besides, the benchmarking RTO had clearly identified problems and clearly defined goals. In such cases, developing a set of PIs was also easier. For example, an RTO wanted to reduce the time taken for project selection. The task was to study the internal mechanism for that and compare it with the practices in the WAITRO study. An indicator that was suggested was the number of steps involved in the evaluation of project proposals. The objective was to reduce the number of steps without compromising the involvement of different stakeholders.

With all its limitations, the WAITRO study should be able to serve two important purposes for the restructuring of the RTOs. First, it can serve as a reference or source material for practices. Second, it can serve as a methodological guide for undertaking a benchmarking exercise. In the following chapters, the study has been used extensively to articulate the problems of organizational restructuring of the RTOs, and how to use the benchmarking technique for the solution of problems.

4
Effectiveness of RTOs

Research and Technology Organizations (RTOs) are in the business of generation and dissemination of knowledge. Even in this business, there is a distinction between research in a particular science discipline and industrial research. Industrial research is a branch of scientific research oriented to applications in the industrial production system. The tag 'applications in the industrial production system' makes industrial research far more complex than pure scientific research. The combustion potential of fossil fuel is a scientific discovery. To make it work together with various other scientific principles for moving a motorcar is the first step towards industrial research. Subsequently, the success in laboratory experiments has to be made to work on the shop floor and then for mass production. The process becomes more and more complex as many scientific principles work together. When it comes to production, scientific and technological principles have to work with a variety of other factors outside the realm of scientific and technological experiments in the laboratory.[5]

For understanding the organizational problems of the RTOs we have to note two important distinctions. The first is regarding dissemination of knowledge. In pure scientific research, that is, when R&D is not particularly oriented towards industrial applications, generated knowledge is considered disseminated enough if it is brought to the knowledge of the peers and the scientific fraternity. In the case of industrial research, dissemination means that knowledge reaches the production stage. New knowledge does not reach the production stage automatically. Nor does the need for new knowledge from the production process automatically create new knowledge. Neither is the adoption of new knowledge in the production system instantaneous, nor is the creation of new knowledge, that is R&D, immediate. RTOs work as interfaces between the two systems.

The second point of distinction is the time factor. Take the example of motor car production again. It has been a long process from fossil fuel to the modern motor car through thousands of incremental innovations over several decades. The basic idea behind the creation and patronage of an RTO is to shorten the time duration of the process of development of a new product. In other words, instead of leaving scientific and technological development to its natural, unknown, and uncertain course, activities have to be organized in such a way that maximum benefit is derived from the present knowledge base in the shortest possible time duration. It is the act of shortening the time duration for exploiting scientific knowledge that creates the need for organization. The RTOs, therefore, can be seen as planned interventions in the natural course of generation and exploitation of knowledge. It is in this context that the effectiveness of an RTO needs to be examined.

Defining effectiveness[6]

The effectiveness of an RTO's activities has to have an inter-temporal dimension over the present and the future. Activities that are considered effective in today's context may not remain effective in the future. An ability to meet the current needs of client industries, therefore, is only a partial account of the effectiveness of an RTO's activities. In a comprehensive sense, effectiveness has to be understood in terms of an RTO's ability to address the future and the technological needs of client industries.

It is tempting to define the effectiveness of an RTO in terms of meeting the day-to-day demands of clients. Going by this definition of effectiveness, if the industry's demand is at a very low level, the RTO's activity will be considered effective if it also operates at the same low level of generation and dissemination of knowledge. That is definitely not effectiveness. Furthermore, tomorrow, if the industry plans to go for higher levels of technological innovations, the RTO will not be able to address its new requirements because the generation of knowledge is not instantaneously responsive to technological needs.

To remain effective, therefore, simply means that an RTO has to remain steps ahead of its clients in terms of level of knowledge. It also needs to be in a state of preparedness to be able to address the future needs of industries. This, of course, has to be in conjunction with the present technological services to industries.

Another important aspect of industrial technology research is that there is no market mechanism by which demand and supply for technological knowledge can be made to meet each other. A rise in the market prices of commodities pushes their demand down to keep the prices at an acceptable level at which supply will be equal to demand. In the case of technological knowledge, market prices will be there only for those technologies, which are commonly known. By definition, advanced knowledge will not have a ready price tag attached to it. Such services are not available as ready-to-use packaged products. They are generally human-resource-embodied. A long and close interaction between the RTOs and industry clients generates confidence and motivates industries to access such services. This then determines prices. The market mechanism is superseded by the organizational mechanism for understanding the present and future demand pattern of industries and gearing up the knowledge-generating system accordingly. Organizational arrangement and practices, therefore, are crucial issues for the effectiveness of RTO activities.

In the next section, we present a model on the basis of this line of understanding. The main purpose of the model is to identify the conditions under which an RTO's activities are supposed to be effective. We shall use these conditions to examine the efficacy of the present organizational arrangements and the practices of RTOs.

A. Conditions for effective RTO services

The demand for technological knowledge by industries is the result of innovative activities undertaken by them. It can be assumed, without being unrealistic, that

$$DK_I = DK_I(T_I); \quad \text{where } \frac{d(K_I)}{d(T_I)} > 0 \tag{1}$$

where DK_I is demand for knowledge from the industry; and T_I is technological innovation by the industry.

RTOs are engaged in the generation and dissemination of technological knowledge to client industries. An RTO's ability to supply technological knowledge will depend upon the existing knowledge level, which has been acquired by the RTO by its earlier knowledge-generation activities. We, therefore, can write $SK_{RTO} = DK_I(GK_{RTO})$ where

$$\frac{d(SK_{RTO})}{d(GK_{RTO})} > 0 \tag{2}$$

where SK_{RTO} = supply of knowledge by the RTO; and GK_{RTO} = generation of knowledge by the RTO.

There is no mechanism by which demand and supply of knowledge can automatically respond to each other. The industry undertakes innovations that need different kinds of technological knowledge. The industry's assessment of an RTO's capabilities, reliability of services, and the extent of RTO–industry interactions will decide which technological needs the industry will access from the RTO.

Now, at any point of time, $DK_I = SK_{RTO}$ will mean that at an existing gap in the knowledge of the industry and the RTO, DK_I is demanded by the industry, and SK_{RTO} is what can be supplied by the RTO. In other words, at any point of time, $DK_I = SK_{RTO}$ at a given level of knowledge gap between the industry and the RTO. Figure 4.1 depicts this proposition.

In Figure 4.1, relations (1) and (2) are superimposed on the same axis. On the X-axis, $DK_I = SK_{RTO}$. The Y-axis, measures both T_I and GK_{RTO}. At point D on X-axis, we get innovations level (T_I) from the $DK_I(T_I)$ curve, and the knowledge level of the RTO (GK_{RTO}) from the SK_{RTO} (GK_{RTO}) curve. The distance between P_3 and P_2 is the gap between knowledge-generation and its application in the form of innovation.

At the point P_1, $T_I = GK_{RTO}$ implying that there is no knowledge gap between the need for innovation and the knowledge generated by an RTO. Thus, both the industry and the RTO are operating at the same knowledge level. Below point P_1, the industry's knowledge level is higher than that of the RTO.

The industry's demand for knowledge from the RTO will critically depend on the knowledge gap. Assuming this primary condition, we can write $DK_I(T_I) = T \times GK_{TRA}$, where '$T$' denotes the knowledge gap.

$$\text{If } \frac{d(T_I)}{dt} \gtreqless 0, \quad \text{then} \quad \frac{d(GK_{RTO})}{dt} \times \frac{1}{GK_{RTO}} \gtreqless \frac{d(DK_I)}{dt} \times \frac{1}{DK_I} \tag{3}$$

This is the primary condition for the effectiveness of an RTO's activities. We can derive the following implications from this condition.

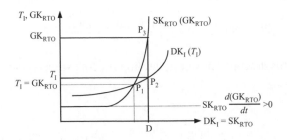

Figure 4.1 Demand–supply dynamics of technological knowledge

B.   Services and R&D activities of the RTOs

At different stages of 'T', the industry–RTO interaction would be at different levels. Knowledge-generation and services offered by the RTOs can broadly be divided into three types.

1. *Ordinary Technological Services*   The knowledge base required for such services is part of the common knowledge base of the industry. An RTO still provides such services because of the infrastructure facility it has developed over time as part of its knowledge-generation activities. Much of the knowledge required for these services is embodied in the equipment or physical resources in the possession of the RTO. Industry clients access these services because it is cheaper than owning and maintaining these services in-house. We include testing, certification, normal consultancy, training and so on, in this category and call it SCK_{RTO}. It is not functionally related to GK_{RTO}.

2. *Advance Technological Services*   The RTOs also provide advance technological knowledge to the industry. Such services are based on advance knowledge generated by RTOs in an earlier period. Let us call it $SAK_{RTO} = SAK_{RTO}(GK_{RTO})$.

3. *Generation of Basic Knowledge*   Part of the knowledge generated is not immediately demanded by the industry because the same may not be of use at the present level of the innovation plan of the industry. This kind of knowledge can be called SBK_{RTO}; or basic knowledge generated by the RTOs. We can write that $SBK_{RTO} = SBK_{RTO}(GK_{RTO})$. The basic knowledge generated by the RTO is beyond the scope of the foreseeable innovation plan of the industries. The form of output of such activities is mainly publications and patents. We can, therefore, write,

$$GK_{RTO} = SCK_{RTO} + SAK_{RTO} + SBK_{RTO} \tag{4}$$

where $(SCK_{RTO})_t = f(GK_{RTO})_{t-i}$,   and, $\dfrac{d(SCK_{RTO})_t}{d(GK_{RTO})_t} = 0$,

$$SAK_{RTO} = DK_I = DK_I(T_I), \quad \text{so} \quad \frac{d(SAK_{RTO})}{dt} = \frac{d(DK_I)}{dt}$$

Based on this description we can develop the following scenarios.

Scenario 1

If, $\dfrac{d(GK_{RTO})}{dt} > 0$ and $\dfrac{d(DK_I)}{dt} \leqslant 0$,   then, $\dfrac{d(GK_{RTO})}{dt} \leqslant \dfrac{d(SBK_{RTO})}{dt}$ (5)

This means that when the demand for knowledge from the RTO is declining or unchanged, the RTO's knowledge-generation activities will be more basic in nature. This will create a wider gap between the knowledge level of RTOs and the industry, resulting in a reduced level of interaction.

Scenario 2

$$\frac{d(DK_I)}{dt} = D_1 \times \frac{d(SCK_{RTO})}{dt} + D_2 \times \frac{d(SAK_{RTO})}{dt} + D_3 \times \frac{d(SBK_{RTO})}{dt} > 0 \quad (6)$$

now, since $\dfrac{d(SAK_{RTO})}{dt} < 0$ and $\dfrac{d(SBK_{RTO})}{dt} < 0,$

so $\dfrac{d(DK_I)}{dt} = D_1 \dfrac{d(SCK_{RTO})}{dt} > 0$ \quad (7)

This means that in a situation where the knowledge gap is reverse in favour of industries, the demand for RTO services will be restricted only to the common services provided by the RTO. This would widen the gap in interaction between the RTO and the industry.

C. Human resources of the RTOs

The knowledge generated by the RTOs can be written as

$$GK_{RTO} = HR_{RTO} + PR_{RTO} \quad (8)$$

HR_{RTO} is the human-resource-embodied knowledge and PR_{RTO} is the physical-resource-embodied knowledge of the RTOs.

Similarly, the knowledge available with the industries is,

$$GK_I = HR_I + PR_I \quad (9)$$

Total HR available in the knowledge system as a whole is

$$HR = HR_I = HR_{RTO} \quad \text{or} \quad HR_I = HR - HR_{RTO} \quad (10)$$

Technological innovation by the industries will increase the demand for HR_I.

of, $\dfrac{d(GK_{RTO})}{dt} < 0$

then $\dfrac{d(HR_I)}{dT_I} \dfrac{dT_I}{dt} = \dfrac{dHR}{dt} (= 0) - \dfrac{d(HR_{RTO})}{d(GK_{RTO})} \times \dfrac{d(GK_{RTO})}{dt}$ \quad (11) or, whatever is the loss of HR for RTOs will be the gain of the industries.

$$\frac{d(\text{GK}_{\text{RTO}})}{dt} = \frac{d(\text{HR}_{\text{RTO}})}{dt} + \frac{d(\text{PR}_{\text{RTO}})}{dt} \quad \text{if} \quad \frac{d(\text{HR}_{\text{RTO}})}{dt} \leqslant 0 \tag{12}$$

The addition to the knowledge of an RTO is only in terms of its physical resources or in terms of equipment and machinery. This result is quite consistent with the earlier finding where we have seen that when the industry's knowledge level is higher than that of the RTO, the RTO's services remain restricted only to testing, certification and so on, which are equipment- or machine-embodied knowledge.

D.   Self-sustainability

We have assumed zero supply cost for the RTO's services to the industry. From equation (4) we can write

$$E \times \text{GK}_{\text{RTO}} = E_1 \text{SCK}_{\text{RTO}} + E_2 \text{SAK}_{\text{RTO}} + E_3 \text{SBK}_{\text{RTO}} \tag{13}$$

where E is the expenditure of GK_{RTO}, E_1 is the maintenance expenditure for common equipment-based services, E_2 is the expenditure for applied knowledge, and E_3 is the same for R&D in advanced areas.

Similarly, revenue earned is

$$R \times \text{GK}_{\text{RTO}} = R_1 \text{SCK}_{\text{RTO}} + R_2 \text{SAK}_{\text{RTO}} + R_3 \text{SBK}_{\text{RTO}} \tag{14}$$

R_3 being 0

$$E_3 \text{SBK}_{\text{RTO}} = (R_1 - E_1) \text{SCK}_{\text{RTO}} + (R_2 - E_2) \text{SAK}_{\text{RTO}}$$

or

$$E_3 \frac{d(\text{SBK}_{\text{RTO}})}{dt} = (R_1 - E_1) \frac{d(\text{SCK}_{\text{RTO}})}{dt} + (R_2 - E_2) \frac{d(\text{SAK}_{\text{RTO}})}{dt} \tag{15}$$

Now, to sustain $\dfrac{d(\text{SBK}_{\text{RTO}})}{dt} > 0$

$\dfrac{d(\text{SAK}_{\text{RTO}})}{dt} > 0$, which is when $\dfrac{d(T_1)}{dt} > 0$, and $\dfrac{d(\text{SCK}_{\text{RTO}})}{dt} > 0$

For RTOs $\dfrac{d(T_1)}{dt} < 0$ may occur in two ways:

1. When the industry is innovative but the system is open enough for it to access technological knowledge from sources other than the RTOs;
2. When the industry is not innovative enough to place a demand for technological knowledge from the RTOs.

In both cases, the industry will still access the SCK_{RTO} component of services from the RTOs. This segment, therefore, has to generate enough revenue so that $\dfrac{d(SBK_{RTO})}{dt} > 0$, and the RTOs make an effort only to build up physical-resource-based capability.

If this segment fails to do so, then,

$$\frac{d(SBK_{RTO})}{dt} < 0, \quad \text{resulting} \quad \frac{d(SAK_{RTO})}{dt} < 0,$$

to arrive at a situation where,

$$\frac{d(SBK_{RTO})}{dt} < 0, \quad \text{but } \frac{d(T_I)}{dt} > 0 \tag{16}$$

and perpetuate this relation to the extent of irrelevance of the RTOs as a system of knowledge-generation and engaged only as a centre for providing minor technical services.

Crux of the model

We have postulated that at any point of equality between the industries' demand for technological knowledge and supply of the same by the RTOs, there is an accompanying knowledge gap between the RTOs and their clients. The RTOs need to fulfil this basic condition.

Services can be of two types: one, predominantly physical-resource-based; and two, predominantly human-resource-based. The clients will restrict their demands to physical-resource-based services if there is no gap in the knowledge base embodied in the human resources of the RTOs and their clients. It would tend to be the same if the clients' knowledge base is higher, or if it is too low compared to the RTOs'. If the knowledge base is embodied in physical resources, clients may continue to access the RTOs' resources in either case since it may be more cost-effective than possessing all kinds of equipment (physical resources).

The core issue of this presentation is the knowledge gap between the RTOs and the industry. If the gap is too big in favour of the RTOs, that is, demand from the industries is too low compared to the capability of the RTOs, the knowledge base of the RTO will be perceived to be redundant. This will resemble a situation where a modern R&D structure is super-imposed on an archaic industrial system. Many developing countries, in fact, face this problem. Erstwhile colonies in Asia and Africa, which emulated the R&D organization models of Europe (mainly the British model of state patronage of scientific and industrial research), in particular, are facing this problem. Laboratories were generally accused of being unconcerned with the industries' needs. In such cases, the RTOs' services to the industries remained generally restricted to routine services like testing, calibration, certification and so on.

On the other hand, if the gap is in favour of the industry's clients, the industry will not find it useful enough for its technological needs and growth. We have defined the RTOs' present services to the industry as the fruit of accumulated past knowledge. Lagging behind the knowledge base of the industry means that, somewhere in the process, the RTOs have stopped acquiring new knowledge that would be embodied in the human resources. They may still retain services based on their physical resources for two main reasons. First, a client may prefer to use the facilities provided by an RTO to minimize the cost of acquiring equipment. In fact, it may choose to develop different sets of equipment from those available with the RTO and complement its services with in-house facilities. Second, in many cases, most of the public-funded RTOs are empowered with statutory technical services that are mandatory for the clients. The clients, therefore, have to access the technical services of the RTOs that are essentially physical-resource-based.

There is an intangible trap here. At any point of time, if these circumstances are in the nature of the clients' demands, and if the RTOs are unwittingly led by the demand of the clients, they will turn out to be an organization without much human resources and knowledge-generation. As present services offered by the RTOs are due to accumulated past knowledge, the absence of knowledge-generation activity at any point of time will lead to a lack of anything to offer in the future. Another fallout of this process will be a loss of human resources for the RTOs. Thus, the RTOs will become increasingly unable to retain their human resources and clients will gain at the cost of the RTOs. If the process continues, the knowledge gap between the RTOs and their clients would increase in favour of the clients, finally making the RTOs totally redundant.

Add the condition of self-sustainability to the condition where the RTOs have depleted human resources and the industries' demands for services are restricted to physical-resource-based services, and we shall arrive at a situation where the RTOs are moving further and further down the knowledge chain. This means that instead of generating new knowledge, the RTOs will gradually relegate themselves to minor technical services at the bottom of the knowledge chain.

Measuring R&D effectiveness

The available literature on the measurement of R&D effectiveness generally deals with the R&D activities of the corporate sector. The problem of R&D effectiveness of the RTOs has failed to receive similar attention from researchers.

Szakonyi (1994) has presented an excellent review of various measures of R&D effectiveness. He has convincingly argued that most of the measures actually deal with R&D output or outcome rather than effectiveness. He reviewed literature of the last 30 years. This review enabled him to identify the main constituents of R&D effectiveness. Based on the broad consensus found in the literature, he has developed a new approach for measuring R&D effectiveness. The emphasis of this approach is on the management of critical functions related to R&D.

Szakonyi, however, dealt only with corporate R&D and, therefore, did not have to struggle with the ends with which the effectiveness of R&D is related. In the case of corporate R&D, effectiveness is finally to be matched with the profit/sales/market share targets of the company. In his approach, the output measure of R&D is complementary to measuring effectiveness. Together they indicate the changes required in the organizational processes of the critical functions of R&D, that is, 'to learn where it stands and how it might improve'.

In the case of non-corporate R&D, the problem is much more complex. The business plan of the potential client industry and the R&D priorities of the RTOs are structurally and organizationally independent. The emphasis on market-driven R&D by RTOs would, therefore, mean institutionalization of linkages with the client industry sector in a suitable organizational structure. Williamson (1995) has argued elaborately about the complex situation arising out of inter-organizational linkages mainly in terms of settlement of disputes. Intra-organizational disputes can be settled within the organizational hierarchy – by fiat of the superior hierarchical level as a last resort. Linkages between organizations are not easy or automatic since the benefit from such a partnership is not always certain, tangible, or easy to assess. It is much more difficult in a typical developing country where R&D is not an integral part of the industrial culture and technological competitiveness is not the rule of the business. The result has been an increasing distance between the RTOs and their potential clients from industries.

The R&D department of a company, on the other hand, is as distant from the other departments as marketing is from production. However, all the departments of a company finally have to function in coordination with each other as guided by the requirements of overall business planning. All the departments have to function under one management body and the managerial environment within the boundary of a company. It is part of the marketing department's responsibility to provide feedback from the market to the production unit. Similarly, the production department for its own sake has to interact with the R&D department. Making these interactions work back and forth, detecting problems in inter-departmental interactions and taking appropriate corrective measures are problems that should be resolved within the managerial hierarchy of a company.

The same is not true for interaction between RTOs and industries – each having their own business boundary and managerial environment. Taking the cue from Bell's (1993) study of historic genesis of RTOs, one can see a kind of elitism in their work culture. Most of them are often referred to as premier institutes of science and technology research where government patronage is taken for granted. These institutions, as far as accountability for their performance is concerned, enjoy an autonomous status. They are accountable only along the line of organizational hierarchy and not to the users of their R&D results. In sociological theory, autonomy has been contrasted with interdependence through inter-organizational linkages. Gouldner had argued that maximizing organizational autonomy would go against establishing organizational interdependence (Gouldner 1959).

The assumption behind the creation of these RTOs is that when a pool of R&D infrastructure and skilled manpower are made available, industries automatically make full use of these resources. The banality of such an assumption is apparent in Bell's historic account of the genesis of the RTOs. In his study, Bell has described how in developed countries, RTOs have grown incrementally on the basis of the objective conditions provided by growing technological competitiveness among industries. On the contrary, in the case of developing countries the same organizational structure has been imitated although similar objective conditions were not present. Over the years, these institutes have preferred to define their R&D problems on their own without any formal or informal interaction with the potential user. Half-hearted efforts are made for the transfer of technologies, if any, developed at the laboratory level. The overall system has been to pass on off-the-shelf technology to industries without any follow-up services. The elitist culture in the RTOs coupled with the non-motivated industries creates an unbridgeable gap between RTOs and industries in developing countries. Briefly, the situation can be described as a dichotomous relation between a non-motivated business organization on the one side and RTOs with considerable R&D infrastructure developed under the largesse of the government on the other.

Forging an organizational link between two different entities is altogether different from linking the different departments within a company. While the latter can be tackled by managerial solutions within an organization, the former is more demanding in terms of total organizational re-engineering. Williamson has elaborately explained these differences in transactions within an organization and those between organizations. In both the cases, however, one can have benchmarks of best practices. While the benchmark for the latter would be a search of the best managerial practices, the benchmark for the former would be the best organizational process that would hold the managerial practices together. There is a distinction in the sense that managerial practices are held within an organizational structure consisting of various organizational processes that are more permanent in nature and less amenable to frequent changes. Managerial practices, on the other hand, are meant to change as and when dictated by the goal of the organization.

Organizational attributes of effectiveness

For the present purpose, our focus is on the organizational processes of an RTO from the perspective of making it more client- or market-oriented. This calls for a business process approach. Cheese and Whelan have characterized such an RTO as 'lean, flexible, constantly learning, constantly adapting itself to the needs of its customers over its life time' (Cheese and Whelan 1996). Benchmarking would mean an identification of organizational processes that are critical to developing closer and more effective interactions between an RTO and its clients.

The problem is one of making RTOs more effective in their R&D performance. In other words, they need to be oriented towards the changing needs of the target client industry. This policy is commonly known as market-driven R&D. Several reports and monographs have been prepared on RTOs under the sponsorship of UNDP, UNIDO, UNCTAD, IDRC and so on. They have suggested that the absence of close interaction with industries (or the absence of a market-driven R&D thrust) is a major weak link in the activities of RTOs. The problem, therefore, is not only to measure how effective their R&D is, but also how to make it more effective. The solution of this problem lies in understanding the industry's needs, translating them into an R&D problem, having the right kind of trained personnel for undertaking R&D, an efficient R&D

management, and finally transferring the R&D results to the production system within real time. In other words, market-driven R&D encompasses all the aspects of the organization of R&D.

Thus, appropriate organizational arrangements have to be in place for the sustenance and growth of an RTO that will create the need, generate, and disseminate knowledge in such a way that it does not need aid to survive. Several organizational attributes that are functionally related to the effectiveness of RTOs (as detailed in the preceding paragraphs) can be located and scrutinized for their efficiency. For the present purpose, we will take up a few core processes that have a direct bearing on the effectiveness of an RTO.

Service: RTOs as organizations have to ensure that there is a balance in the services offered by them. These services have to be complementary to each other. What is the right balance? How can the correct service mix be selected? The organizational process followed for this will have a considerable bearing on the RTO's credibility and effectiveness.

Linkages and interaction with clients: Imagine an RTO that has a service mix to offer to a set of unknown clients – unknown because the RTO does not have much interaction with prospective clients. It waits for clients to come and use its services. Nothing is sure in this situation. A particular RTO's services may or may not be useful for its target clients. The clients may or may not be aware of the credibility and reliability of the RTO's services. Much of this confusion can be allayed and lack of information can be managed by an appropriate mechanism of linkages between clients and RTOs. The RTOs, therefore, have to have organizational arrangements to ensure that linkages with the clients provide both feedback and partnership.

Human resources: Human resources do not simply mean qualified manpower. As argued earlier, in the business of knowledge-generation, the human resources available to an RTO hold the key for its survival in the long term. The development of human resources and making these resources available to the organization has to be a continuous endeavour.

Information flow: An organization's capacity to survive and grow critically depends on its capacity to access, process, and use information for the generation of knowledge and then marketing this knowledge. In other words, efficiency in managing information for the given strategic goal of an organization is the key parameter of success of an organization.

Compare these organizational processes with the list of core RTO processes studied in the WAITRO project as given in the Annexure. The WAITRO study divided an RTO into ten core processes, each process having several sub-processes. We have taken up only four. It is to be noted here that the ten core processes in the WAITRO study are for a comprehensive and generalized characterization of the organization of RTOs. Our study focuses more on studying the organizational attributes that directly influence the effectiveness of an RTO. It is, therefore, to be noted that many of the processes and sub-processes in the WAITRO study are accommodated or integrated in the processes we have identified for our specific purpose.

5
RTO Practices for Effectiveness

In the previous chapter we constructed four major processes that together, we have argued, would influence the effectiveness of RTO services. To recapitulate, those four processes are as follows:

Service: The types of services provided by the RTOs and how the RTO service mix is selected?

Linkages and interaction with clients: How does the RTO come to know and articulate the technological problems of clients.

Human resources: The RTO endeavour for development of human resources and making those resources available to the organization.

Information flow: RTOs' efficiency in managing information for the given strategic goal.

All the above processes are, in fact, an amalgamation of a few function-ally related processes. Let us call them sub-processes. Sub-processes become distinct from each other when they need organizational set-ups that are different. Sub-processes are grouped together to form a process when they together contribute to make the process function. For the present purpose, we shall restrict ourselves to the analysis of a few sub-processes, as we shall argue that they are important components of the chosen processes. In the present chapter, we shall only elaborate the practices. The choice of best practices will be taken up separately in the next chapter.

Process: Service

We have broadly divided RTO activities into three groups. They are basic research, applied research and technical services like training, testing, certifications and so on. Basic research activities are essentially for enhancing the knowledge base of the RTO and may not be of immediate use given the present level of innovation activities of the industry clients. At the same time, these activities prepare the RTO for planning the future services and educating the clients accordingly[7] (Mrinalini 1991). Application oriented research activities are directed to ongoing needs and demands of the client industries. The mainstay of such activities is the accumulated knowledge of the RTO. The accumulated knowledge base is created by basic research undertaken earlier and also by the experience of applied research completed. Technical services are ongoing regular and routine activities of RTOs. In many cases such activities are statutory in nature and mandatory on the part of the clients.

Ideally, the process functions by defining a service mix or relative emphasis of three activities mentioned above. While deciding about the service mix the RTO will have to take care of the present and future needs of the clients. This means that the RTO has to have practices to identify the need of clients and track the courses of future changes. While doing all these the RTO also have to ensure the quality of services provided by them. This is what builds up RTOs' credibility and trust *vis-à-vis* its clients. Regarding RTO practices, questions, therefore, are what is the service mix followed by the RTO; how does it identify clients' (individual or a group of clients) needs; what does it do to ensure the quality of services? We shall study the RTO practices under these broad headings. Details of practices from WAITRO study are given in the Annexure.

Practices for service mix

If we consult the practices under the same heading in the annexure we can observe a few broad types and trends. In the WAITRO samples of RTOs there were no RTO totally devoted to basic research, but there are a few RTOs that devote a fair amount of resources for basic research. The range of practices in this regard is widely diversified; from RTOs fully devoted to providing technical services to highly diversified activities of all types. Most of the RTOs that are mainly devoted to providing technical services like testing, certification, training and so on are created and run by government departments. Such RTOs are mainly found in the developing countries of Asia.

Practices listed above, however, suggest a static scenario. Today's practices have actually evolved over the lifetime of a RTO and should be read as various ways of responding to challenges faced by them. There are RTOs that actually began as testing centres and gradually changed their service profile towards industrial technology development and thereafter to basic research in the areas like new materials. Such a shift in service profile has been associated with the change in client profile from predominantly local small enterprises to international clients from developed countries (The Singapore Institute of Standards and Industrial Research or SISIR is a typical case). On the other hand there are RTOs that started with an appropriate mix of services and activities ranging from basic and applied research to ordinary technical services to clients, but under pressure for revenue generation gradually became service centres (Eight Textile Research Associations in India). At the same time, there are RTOs that have not shown any change in the service or activity profile over their long lifetime (Regional Testing Centres, Small Industry Service Institutes, both from India). Such organizations are seen mainly in developing countries of Asia, Africa and Latin America, and generally established and run by government departments.

Practices for determination of service mix to be offered

The evolution of service or activity profile over time is dependent on the RTOs' ability to recognize and forecast incoming changes. Once the need for changes is recognized RTOs have to have organizational practices in place to bring in necessary changes in services and activities. How do RTOs determine the service mix? The broad categories of practices found in WAITRO study are, market pull, technology push, policy push, RTO management's independent decision, and through informal contacts with the clients. Market pull is the practice where RTOs organize direct interactions with clients, or undertake market research and consult potential clients before designing the service mix to be offered by them. In the case of practices dependent on technology push, services are determined on the basis of the RTOs' own capabilities. In such cases it is quite possible that many of the RTO services may not match market needs. There are cases where RTO services are determined by the policies of the national or local government. These are called policy pushed practices for determination of service mix. In such cases, the RTOs will have much less flexibility or authority to chart their own courses for determining service mix. There are practices where the RTOs' management decide about the service mix and there has been no organizational mechanism to reflect the needs of the clients. These are the examples of practices where the RTOs function in an autonomous fashion *vis-à-vis* their clients.

Practices for ensuring service quality

There are ten distinct practices identified in the WAITRO study for ensuring quality of services offered by RTOs. The range is wide and covers practices like 'not bothered' and active organization mode. In cases where RTOs do not have any organizational arrangements for ensuring quality, services are mostly subsidized or statutory requirements for clients. As opposed to it, there are cases where RTOs assume that since clients are still paying for the services they must be satisfied, so no extra care is needed. In both the cases, there is no organizational mechanism followed for ensuring the quality of services. Among the organizational arrangements for ensuring quality of services there are quite a few ways of getting feedback from clients and translating those into organizational measures. Client satisfaction survey is an important mode in the RTOs of South and North America. Many of the Asian RTOs, particularly prefectural laboratories in Japan, have practices like regular interactions with clients on the issues related to quality of services. The American and European practice is mainly to acquire quality certification for the RTO and its services under recognized quality programmes. Follow up visits after, or, demonstration of results to clients before the delivery is also practised by some Asian and American RTOs. There is also a unique practice like client participating with RTO staff on RTO activities for specific clients.

It has been noticed that the RTOs' choice of practices in this regard is greatly influenced by the types of client groups and the degree of dependence of the RTOs on clients for sustenance. In cases where RTOs serve a wide array of clients from different industry segments of different sizes, or, in other words, where target clients are not strictly defined, RTOs tend to have mainly internal arrangements for quality assurance of their services. In many cases, such arrangements remain dormant or become routine rituals because appropriate logistics for closer interaction with the wide array of clients entail high administrative cost. Closer contacts with clients are easier for RTOs that are supposed to serve a particular industry or technology (e.g. paint industry or electronic engineering). It has also been noticed that as pressure increased on the RTOs to become more self-dependent, that is, to become more dependent on revenue earned from clients, the RTOs went for varieties of organizational arrangements for getting feedback from clients.

Process: Linkages and interaction with clients

In Chapter 2, we made a distinction between corporate and non-corporate R&D. We have argued that the problem of linkages and interaction with the clients or users of the R&D has been intrinsic in non-corporate R&D organizations. The problem has been more pronounced in the case of developing countries that emulated the R&D organization structure from the developed countries, but did not have the comparable technological dynamism of the industries. It has also been argued that, although to a lesser extent, similar problems are not unknown in developed countries as well.

The weak link between R&D and industry could be the result of many other organizational failures. The industry might lose interest in the RTOs because the RTOs did not have the right human or physical resources. The emphasis, therefore, is on the process of human resource and physical resource development. This process could be constrained by inappropriate planning or non-availability of financial resources. Is the financial crunch related to ownership pattern of the RTOs? Or, does it indicate that a change is required in terms of source of funding RTO activities? Are the RTOs facing a problem of depleting human resources over the years because of lack of resources for retaining the best manpower and procuring the best equipment? It is also possible that although the RTOs have the right resources in place they are unable to arouse the confidence of the industries for inappropriate delivery mechanism resulting in time and cost over run. This could be because of poor R&D project management by the RTOs. On many occasions, the industries may not be able to articulate their business problem as a technological problem. In such cases, a proactive RTO is needed to take the initiative to appraise industries about the possible technological solutions for the problem. There are cases where linkage between industries and RTOs was found to be dormant in the sense that industries had been actively using regular routine services provided by the RTOs but in terms of R&D activities they had no commitment. In such cases, the RTO may develop a bias towards developing physical resource-based services sacrificing its human resource advantage. Such a situation may finally be self-defeating for the organization.[8]

Linkages and interaction with clients, therefore, is not adequately attended by having a liaison department in an RTO. Such linkages and interactions address two important issues; the RTO makes its capability known to clients and funders, and also the RTO becomes aware of clients' needs and future strategies. This is in addition to the clients' feedback about the quality of services discussed above. Practices observed by the WAITRO study, in this regard, are discussed below.

Practices for making RTO capability known or, awareness creation strategy

In the annexure on practices there is a long list of practices under the same heading. All the RTOs studied have these practices in some form or other. RTOs, those are supply led, that is, those who have mandated to provide some services to a targeted beneficiary (not client[9]) group, are generally lackadaisical about building awareness of their programmes and capabilities. They will have many practices on paper but most of them would not have been practised in reality. RTOs engaged mainly in providing technical services and not doing much of technological research do not have practices related to international awareness or attracting international clients. In general, more varieties in practices are found in RTOs that have to generate resources for their sustenance and depend on services to clients. This is, however, not true in the case of the prefectural laboratories of Japan. These laboratories, although they have full funding from the government sources, have aggressive awareness building practices. Other than many of the practices listed, a common practice of these laboratories, but unique in a general context, is to provide free on-site consultancy to clients.

Identification of clients' needs

RTOs have to have a mechanism to identify and foresee clients needs and design their services accordingly. Clients' needs and RTOs' responses to them would be of two types; needs of a group of clients, and that of an individual client. While the latter is generally a specific demand of a particular client, the former is certain facilities and services of a general nature.

Practices to identify individual client's needs

There are 12 practices identified in the WAITRO study. These practices are used in various combinations by RTOs for reaching the clients and as windows to clients' changing technological needs. With these 12 practices we have to include the practice of having no organizational arrangement and RTOs generally expecting clients to approach them as and when they have needs. The last practice is generally found in some of the RTOs in developing countries of Asia. The other twelve practices are either the direct result of an already built-up RTO reputation with clients or are efforts to build up trust with clients. Thus, the RTO personnel's representations on clients' boards or other forums, or participation in designing clients' strategic planning is a reflection of the RTOs' reputation and trustworthiness with clients. On the other hand, regular visits to clients, manpower exchange programmes and free on-site consultancy are direct methods to develop intimate relations with clients. Practices like contacts through RTO-trained personnel working with clients, training programmes and seminars organized by RTOs, trade fairs, or through routine services provided to the clients are indirect methods and complimentary to other direct methods for building up close contact with clients. The practices of the RTOs, in this regard, are generally a combination of all three categories.

Practices to identify client group's needs

Listed practices again can be divided into two groups; one mainly an internal arrangement and the other through interaction with other stakeholders of RTO services. In the first group, practices vary in terms of involvement of RTO personnel. If in some practices it is RTO senior management deciding the client group's needs, in other cases it is the personnel at junior levels giving the main input. In the second category, various levels of interactions with clients are reflected. These interactions are either through the RTO board where clients are represented, or through regular interactions with clients, or through a separate board where, other than the RTO and client, many other experts take part in decision making. There are RTOs where such decisions are given by the owner (e.g. government) and, therefore, RTO management does not have to do anything in that regard.

Process: Human resources

The importance of human resources for the RTOs' long-term sustenance can not be over emphasized. This is true not only for an R&D organization but also for any organization irrespective of its purpose. An organization, however, is not a uniform entity across time and space. Briefly defined, an organization is a defined arrangement of human resources to work in cooperation with each other and with physical resources for achieving mandated objective(s). The first element in this definition is a set of objectives to be attained. The attainment of the defined objective would need both physical and human resources of various capabilities. Human resources hold the key in an organization because physical resources, although not less important, are inert and are to be operated upon for capitalizing on its capability. It is human resources that have the skill and knowledge of making use of physical resources. In addition, human resources have flexible uses in contrast to physical resources that have rigidly defined capabilities or functions. Knowledge or skill embodied in human resources is not specific to a particular use and the same knowledge base and skill can be used for more than one purpose, in fact, for unlimited purposes. Again, knowledge and skill of human resources can be enhanced, developed and directed. It is the learning capability that distinguishes human resources from other types of resources. For growth and sustenance of a knowledge generating organization, therefore, human resource becomes the singular most important factor.

The assertion about unlimited capability of human resources, however, demands clarification. It is unlimited only when we think of 'human resources' as a pool of synergically related knowledge base and not as an individual human being. Simon (1976) has elaborated on the concept of 'bounded rationality' that broadly means limit of cognitive ability of a human being. As an individual a human being and his/her knowledge base have limited use. An individual becomes part of human resources only when he/she becomes a constituent of a knowledge system. It is in this context that the importance of an organization is to be understood. An organization creates human resources out of individuals by establishing synergy among human-embodied individual skill and knowledge base.

The process of human resource development, therefore, will have constituents like practices for attracting the best and potential manpower and retaining them, career opportunities and opportunities for capability building. Practices identified in the WAITRO study are as follows.

Practices for attracting the best and potential manpower and retaining them

This will have two components; one is for the practices related to hiring manpower and the other is compensation package or practices for retaining the best manpower. Practices for hiring manpower will reflect the long-term strategies of the RTO. One approach could be recruiting manpower and grooming them for the organization having a long-term perspective in mind. Another could be the RTO maintaining a skeletal staff and hiring experts as and when required. They are both formal and informal recruitment practices. Formal and rigid, recruitment practices are generally associated with the RTOs that are part of a government system or heavily dependent on government grants. More flexibility is enjoyed by RTOs that are not directly controlled by the government.

By retaining manpower, RTOs actually retain their knowledge advantage. This is important when an RTO has actually created human resources out of its manpower. Practices related to the creation of human resources will be taken up separately. Again, practices related to retaining manpower have to be accompanied by practices for discharging manpower. In the case of RTOs of developing countries of Asia retention of manpower is by default because once recruited they can be discharged only through such a roundabout way that it is practised only on the rarest of occasions. In most of the RTOs in Asia and Africa, the compensation package is very rigidly defined compared to the practices in European and American RTOs. Most of the Asian and African RTOs are created and heavily dependent on government grants and, therefore, have to follow rigid government systems of compensation packages. In many cases, although the RTOs follow a rigid pay structure, it is complemented with a system of bonus or other performance-based criteria.

Practices for career opportunities

Career opportunities available to employees are also important for the RTOs to be able to retain right human resources. The RTOs have to have a system of identifying the best among the employees and reward them in different ways. What are the practices for performance evaluation of staffs and an associated reward system? In most of the cases evaluation mechanism is actually a part of career advancement opportunities. In American RTOs, however, there are practices for identifying the scope of improvement for individual employees. This responsibility is generally vested with the supervisory staffs of the RTO with some variations in terms of involvement of supervisors across the group and hierarchy. In the case of the prefectural laboratories of Japan the chief of the RTO evaluates the performance and indicates scope for improvement. Rewards are given in the form of citations from the RTO chief for significant performances.

The practice of on-the-job evaluation helps annual performance evaluation of the RTO staff. Annual performance evaluation is done for career advancement of the staff. Career advancement opportunities are widely different in the RTOs. In American RTOs it is based on a performance management system that is fairly quantified. In some of the Asian RTOs staff evaluation is done as an annual performance review and is directly related to promotion to a higher level. In typical Indian RTOs the scope of promotion is time bound based on annual performance evaluation. In the CSIR system promotion is *in situ* and promotion is essentially in terms of monetary benefits. It is not so in other RTOs of Asia where staffs have to compete with each other for superior positions. In Nepal, a percentage of posts are kept for internal promotion and the rest is open for outsiders as well.

Practices for capability-building

It is generally recognized that with competitive compensation packages and career opportunities the RTOs would also have to create opportunities for enhancing the skill and knowledge base of the employees. In this process, the RTOs gain by enriching their human resources and, therefore, prepare for new challenges. It also has implications on retaining the right manpower. In the present world of quick obsolescence of knowledge and faster rate of change of knowledge, it is imperative on scientific and technical manpower to get the opportunity to acquire higher skill and thereby retain the market value. The practices of capability building, therefore, are important for both RTOs and their staffs.

The most important question here is, how the RTOs identify the opportunities of capability-building and staffs to be involved in the process. There are practices of involving external experts and/or involving a group of clients for identification of areas of capability building. In some cases, it is an informal process. Once identified, the personnel to be involved are chosen by the heads or supervisors of the relevant departments. The next question is, how are the capability building programmes made operational? There are six (seven, if we add the practice of having no practice for encouraging capability building of staffs) different types of practices observed in the WAITRO study as listed in the annexure. There are different combinations of practices used by the RTOs.

Process: Information flow

The role of information in modern society can not be over emphasized. In fact, a modern society can be distinguished from a traditional society by information intensity. Information intensity is the extent of accessing, processing and using information. Organizations in modern society can also be defined in terms of informatization. It can be argued that an organization is what it does for accessing, processing and using information. In other words this is what management of information is all about.

According to the latest understanding in management and organization theory, information has long surpassed its traditional role as input for decision making. The traditional theory of organization has seen it as a decision making body that uses information as input for rational choice. This view of organization and use of information has been improved by defining an organization as a sense making body; that is making sense out of information it accesses. Broadly described as *knowledge society*, it has been argued that such societies flourish on generation of knowledge out of information. Drucker (1993) has called knowledge, rather than capital or labour, the only meaningful economic resource of the post-capitalist or knowledge society. Organizations in such societies, therefore, are seen as users of information not only for decision making but also for generating knowledge – the main dynamics of an emerging society.

Information, knowledge and organization

Once such an organization is in place, the knowledge base is enriched by interactions and opens up the opportunity for creation of new knowledge. An organization has to be structured so that it promotes such interactions and becomes conducive to creation of new knowledge because in the long run an organization can survive and grow only if it is a knowledge creating organization. One important structural characteristic of any organization is information flow within the organization. This is essentially a part of information processing activity and also intra-organization cross-accessing of information. An organization, in fact, can be defined in terms of channels of information flow. A network of such channels is the organizational structure. An organization defines the value of the types of information and decides about the course it should follow across the organizational hierarchy. This information can be generated internally or it can be accessed from sources outside the organization. A dynamic organization will have both, or in other words, the organization structure will be so designed that it can access and process information from within as well as from outside the organization.

While flowing across the organizational hierarchy, the accessed information undergoes a metamorphosis with value addition through interpretation. It is in this process that organization takes advantage of human resources by overcoming the problem of 'bounded rationality' and accumulating knowledge input from a resource pool. Organizational efficiency is critically dependent on the extent of value addition in the process of flow of information across the organizational hierarchy.

In the traditional mode of use of organization, such information flow will essentially mean approval or sanction. That is, a file will move up from the bottom for approval from somebody up in the hierarchy. The information will come back to its origin with instructions. This is an example of a bureaucratic organization where human resources and its function is desired to be as rigid as it is in the case of physical resources. Human resources, in such an organization, lose the role of resources and also as a knowledge generating agency. Such organizations will be stable but moribund over time. On the contrary, organizations where there is information flow with value addition, the process of knowledge generation is set into action. Simultaneously, an organizational dynamics is created by which human resources become more enriched, and the organization's quest for more and more information increases. The organization becomes more receptive to accessing information and seeking opportunities for gainful application of generated knowledge. In fact, the application of knowledge itself becomes a part of the process of knowledge generation. Another aspect of the new dynamics is that the organizational structure itself changes along the line of increasing quest for more extensive and intensive knowledge. The organizational structure, therefore, can neither remain stable nor rigid over time. One indicator of a dynamic knowledge creating organization, therefore, is whether the organization has undergone structural changes over time.

Organization for knowledge generation

In the previous section we have argued that a dynamic organization will use its human resources for generation of information and processing of the same for generation of new knowledge. This is true for a firm, a corporate body or for a sports organization and even for a gambling organization. What if we take up an example of an organization where business itself is generation of new knowledge. This means that the organization is mandated to generate and create opportunities for application of new knowledge! When everything discussed above remains true also for such organizations the major point of difference is that such organizations can not afford to be bureaucratic; nor can their structure remain unchanged over a period. The critical distinction of such organizations is that the organizations have something to offer which others do not. Compare this with a firm, which may compete with several other firms selling the same products. An organization in the business of knowledge generation can not sell the same knowledge that another organization is selling. We are talking about R&D organizations. R&D organizations can be characterized as organizations mandated to generation and application of knowledge. It is essentially human resource based and knowledge generated is generally human embodied.

A basic characteristic of such organizations is that they demand extensive access to information and a high degree of informatization. An R&D organization will have to work in a three-world mode. The first world consists of the organizations engaged in knowledge generation. The organization in question has to be abreast about the present and future trends in the world. Then comes the world of knowledge applications where knowledge is finally transformed to be used in the production sphere. The organization in question has to be fully aware of the new possibilities and potentialities of the application of new knowledge and also the possible new applications of existing knowledge. The transformation of knowledge into the field of production is as complex and fuzzy as the generation of knowledge. Success here depends as much on the right partner as on the substance of the knowledge. The third is a world of its own where the organization in question works on the information accessed from the other two worlds, drawing a strategy for pursuing a particular trajectory and field of knowledge keeping the potentiality and capability of the use in the sphere of production. The extent of informatization, that includes information accessing, processing and use, therefore, plays a critical role in an R&D organization. Information management has to be more efficient and intensive in an R&D organization than it is in any other organization dealing with anything which is a derivative of knowledge.

Information flow from the other two worlds and the processing of the same within the RTO organizational structure is, therefore, the lifeline for the functioning of an RTO. The RTOs, therefore, have to have an arrangement of interactions within and with the outside world for accessing, processing and using information. Practices, in this regards, are seen under 'Networking with other technology providers', 'Networking with industry', and 'Internal communications'.

Practices for networking with other technology providers

There are RTOs in Africa and America that do not encourage any networking with other technology providers. This means that there are no formal arrangements. Most of these agencies are government outfits for technology services. Those RTOs that encourage networking follow different courses of activities. In the WAITRO study such activities have been divided between low-cost and high-cost activities. Most of the American, European and Japanese RTOs covered in the study seek high-cost networking activities whereas Asian RTOs go for low-cost activities. It is also to be noticed that most of the low-cost activities are comparatively passive activities. So, when low-cost activities include RTO personnel's representations in universities/technical schools, and encouragement for maintaining close contacts with people of its fields, the high-cost activities include organizing international seminars, making RTO personnel members of professional societies and so on.

Practices for networking with industry

The most commonly found practice is the RTOs' training and other programmes for industry. Industry representation in the RTO board or industry participation in the RTOs' advisory committees is again common.

Also common is RTOs' personnel serving in the industry committees. In a few cases in America and India, RTOs were found creating an effective linkage through the RTO trained personnel working in the industry. In some cases the RTOs create a club as a forum for closer interaction. As members clients from industries get subsidized services from the RTO.

Practices for internal communication

How the information will travel within the organization depends upon the internal structure of the organization. Such a structure, in the case of an RTO, will mean 'Organizational Management Style', 'Grouping of Its Capabilities', 'Responsibility Bestowed to Organizational Units' and its 'Functional Authority Structure'.

There were four broad 'Organizational Management Styles' observed among the RTOs studied. Those were: (a) Hierarchical, centralized decision making, informal relationship, responsibility granted only by the RTO chief based on his perception of the capability of the staff; (b) Hierarchical, centralized decision making, task oriented, formal relationship, management by job description; (c) Non-hierarchical, decentralized decision making, task oriented, responsibility by accomplishment, management by objectives; (d) Decentralized, non-hierarchical, informal relation, responsibility by accomplishment, management by enthusiasm.

The overall style of management also conditions the extent of informatization within an organization. In a typical centralized and hierarchical decision making system, information has to flow through a defined hierarchy and finally end to the chief, who would take all decisions. In a more participatory kind of style, the extent of informatization has to be multi-channeled. Again, granting responsibility to staffs down the line and monitoring accomplishment would demand an information network that would be different from the practice where the RTO chief controls and assesses the accomplishment.

It has been observed that most of the RTOs in Asia, Africa and Latin America are closer to the (a) type of management style. These institutions also have comparatively much less informatization. In European and American RTOs there is a clear shift towards the (c) style of management. In many RTOs of Europe (d) has been tried with noticeable success.

The practices of 'Grouping of RTO capabilities' provide deeper insight into the internal management of an RTO. Practices here are shown in terms of 'traditional academic grouping' (like chemistry, physics, etc.), 'technology grouping' (like electronics, mechanical engineering, etc.), 'industry based grouping' (like leather industry, textile industry, etc.), 'grouping based on service types offered' (like, consultancy, training, etc.), or a combination of all.

A clear trend is in favour of a technology-based grouping. It has a remarkable influence on project and manpower management. Most of the RTOs, where grouping are based on technology, draw manpower from different units for particular projects because most of the projects need expertise of various types and nature. These are the RTOs that are also very well networked with other technology providers. Inter unit collaboration has its implication on information flow within the organization.

Once the manpower of an RTO is grouped in units, what is the level of responsibility given to the groups and what actually are these groups expected to accomplish? Are the groups expected to perform only the given task, whereas the responsibility of cost and revenue rests with the chief? These questions deal with the delegation of authority and responsibility. Here, we have seen practices only in terms of activity centered, activity and cost centered, and activity, cost and revenue centered. Clearly, the last practice grants a wide range of responsibility of trust on the groups. Such a practice has been seen in American RTOs.

From the group level to project level there are three major types of practices in terms of responsibility sharing; the RTO chief managing all projects, heads of divisions managing projects, project leaders chosen based on the nature of projects and expertise needed. The management of a project means forming the project team, financial and manpower management, and the responsibility of delivering the result on time and within cost. Practices here actually show the extent of delegation of authority and the training of the staff for greater responsibility.

All the above practices characterize the interpersonal contacts and responsibility in the internal organization of an RTO. Organizing them in various ways, in effect, structure the information flow within the organization. Essential differences among the practices are in terms of extensity and intensity of information – accessing and processing and adding value to information as it flows.

Besides the above channels through organizational structure, there are other ways for general communications in an organization. These channels are either media based (like, newsletters, magazines, etc.) or social activities based. The basic difference between the structural communication channel and the general communication channel is that the former ensures task and activity related person to person contact, while the latter is more passive and general. There is a list of 25 practices that are used in different combinations by the RTOs in the WAITRO study. There are RTOs that make concerted efforts to build up an effective internal communication system. Such RTOs would try to use the maximum number of channels out of the 25 mentioned in the list. It is interesting to note that among the RTOs in Asian countries internal communication is restricted mainly to division level meetings and meetings with the chiefs.

In this chapter we have delineated a simple course of organizational process for effectiveness of RTO activities. There are many more important processes that significantly contribute to the efficiency of RTO services. We have taken up the simplest course for the sake of convenience and also to narrow down the focus to more critical issues. Many of the processes are actually interspersed with the few chosen here. How detailed should be the processes and practices depends on the ultimate purpose of study. In the present volume we wish to restrict our task to developing an example of organizational best practice for the restructuring of RTOs.

6
Measuring the Effectiveness of RTOs

We have described the practices for a few chosen critical processes of an RTO. These practices have been observed for 60 RTOs all over the world. Is it possible to choose the best practice out of a set of practices related to a process? To qualify the question further, the best practice has to be one that will ensure the effectiveness of an RTO's activities. To be able to deliver a precise answer to the question of best practices, some sort of quantification would be necessary for measuring the performance of practices under a particular process. What we need, therefore, is process-wise performance indicators so that practices can be compared with each other and the best practice can be benchmarked. What would be the right performance indicator and how can we arrive at the appropriate indicator? In the Annexure, along with the sub-process-wise practices, we have also listed the performance indicators used by the WAITRO study and also the best practices arrived at by the study. In this chapter, we shall discuss the issues related to these performance indicators and best practices.

Performance indicators

If we take a close look at the sub-process-wise performance indicators, as given in the Annexure, it will be evident that they constitute mostly the revenue earned, the cost, and the satisfaction of staff, clients, management, and the owner of the RTO. Information related to revenue and cost is easily available from the balance sheet of an RTO. The extent of satisfaction of different stakeholders of an RTO, however, has to be surveyed. In the case of the WAITRO study, such survey-based information was not available, and, hence most of the quantitative information was balance-sheet-based. In the absence of survey-based information, the balance-sheet-based indicators were complemented by the project team's assessment of a practice in terms of its efficiency and contribution to the attainment of the goal of the organization. In some cases, experts' views were solicited for a comparative assessment of a set of practices. An indicative observation on the possible best practices based on this assessment is also presented in the Annexure.

The indicators to be used have to have functional relations with the process or sub-process. For example, let us consider the case of the process called 'service' and its sub-process called 'service mix'. The suggested indicator in this case is the revenue earned from clients. It can be argued that an appropriate service mix will attract more and more clients and, therefore, revenue from clients will show an increasing trend. So, either the number of clients, or the revenue earned from services over a period of time, or both can be indicators for ascertaining the appropriateness of the service mix. Adequate care, however, has to be taken to weed out spurious information. The revenue earned by an RTO over a period of time has to be checked for rise in charges for the same services and the data has to be standardized accordingly to avoid over-estimation. Similarly, for the number of clients, it has to be decided beforehand whether the number of services or the number of clients served would be appropriate for the purpose.

It is quite possible that some of the services offered by an RTO are monopoly services for statutory reasons. In such cases, neither the number of clients nor the increase in revenue earned would be appropriate indicators. Such information, therefore, will have to be complemented with a client satisfaction survey. This survey needs to be a routine task and an integral component of the service itself. There has to be an arrangement for a regular analysis of survey-based information for corrective measures.

Once such information is available and processed, it will be possible to rank all the practices identified with different RTOs. The practice getting the highest rank can be benchmarked as the best practice. This exercise has to be undertaken for every process or sub-process, as the case may be, for developing sub-process-wise performance indicators and best practices. It is quite possible that there will be common indicators for a group of processes or sub-processes. In the example of the sub-process called 'service mix', as shown in the Annexure, we have identified that having a practice of 'providing comprehensive service' is the best practice. Comprehensive service in this case means more or less equal importance to basic, applied, and ordinary technical services. The selected best practice, in this case, appeals to our intuitive reasoning.

But, is this method of developing performance indicators adequate?

Limitations of performance indicators

We began with an assumed functional relationship between the practice for service mix and the revenue earned by an RTO. We expected that an appropriate service mix would attract more satisfied clients and more revenue. Is the reverse also true? That is, if an RTO's revenue earning is increasing, does it mean that it has a good service mix to offer? In the model on the effectiveness of an RTO, in Chapter 4, we derived conditions that related RTO service mix and its effectiveness. The main assured source of revenue for RTOs is routine services. The model suggested how an RTO will be devoid of knowledge advantage *vis-à-vis* the clients if it concentrates more on the generation of revenue in this fashion, and neglects applied and basic research activities. It is, therefore, possible for an RTO to maximize current revenue at the cost of future knowledge advantage. A revenue-based performance indicator may, therefore, be totally misleading for the identification of best practices.[10]

Again, when we are constructing functionality between indicators and a process, we are also assuming a continuous and differentiable function. In reality, neither of these properties can be imposed on organizational processes. Suppose we rank practices in terms of some quantifiable indicators, and say that, practice 'A' scores 5 per cent more than practice 'B'. Will that be sufficient for accepting or rejecting any practice as good or bad?

A practice is a micro-level action in an organization. It works in tandem with many other processes and practices. Balance sheet data, on the other hand, is not practice-specific and reflects the macro-level performance of the organization. Revenue or similar information, therefore, is the result of simultaneous functioning of many practices involving many organizational processes. To estimate the contribution of one particular practice to any organization-level data, we have to control the effect of other practices on the data. Unless that is achieved, it would be inappropriate to choose one practice as an explanatory action only on the basis of practice-wise functional relations. As evident from the WAITRO study too, the same set of indicators is functionally related to many processes. It means that all these processes actually contribute to the balance sheet data – like the revenue earning of an RTO.

Besides this, many processes and practices may actually be passive and decorative. A macro-level performance indicator may, therefore, overestimate its contribution. For example, all RTOs realize the importance of close interaction with their client industries. Many RTOs, therefore, have representatives of the client from industries in their governing board. During the WAITRO study, it was observed that in many cases such a representation of clients is more decorative than active. If macro-level indicators like revenue earned are being used as performance indicators, the effect of the interaction between the RTO and its clients will tend to be overestimated.

Intrinsic property of performance indicators

The set of performance indicators suggested here is an empirical construction. We have actually hypothesized a relationship between a process or a practice and the macro-level performance of an RTO. Even for macro-level performance, we have assumed that the most important aspect of performance is the revenue earned by an RTO. Earning more and more revenue may not be the end objective of an RTO. We have argued that revenue maximization as a primary objective may in fact result in the RTO losing the legitimacy for its very existence. From the model presented in Chapter 4, an RTO can be redefined as an organization engaged in the generation and diffusion of knowledge, and earning enough revenue in the process for infusing the necessary vitality in its present and future activities. Here lies the importance of a process like 'service' and the various sub-processes within it. Many of the organizational processes and practices, therefore are intended to facilitate the uncertain and unknown tract of knowledge. They might contribute to the RTO's revenue in an untraceable or at best in an extremely roundabout way.

An RTO engaged in industrial technology research does not generate knowledge in isolation, nor does it disseminate common knowledge that will maximize its revenue in the short term. It has to be responsive to its clients' demands by exposing them to and providing them with services based on a higher level of knowledge. The two most important components of this task are to become responsive to clients' needs and demands, and to be able to access and process a higher level of knowledge to provide technological services to clients. An RTO's internal organization has to be structured in such a way that it can work as a link between the knowledge world and the clients' world – the production system. What are the basic organizational principles behind the efficiency of an RTO internal organization? Once such principles are identified, the different organizational processes and practices of an RTO have to be examined in that light. Therefore, these principles have to be an intrinsic part of the performance indicators of a practice.

Market versus organization-driven RTO[11]

In economic literature, an organization is seen as an alternative to the market. Any production technology is a part of a knowledge chain. One end of this knowledge chain is part of common knowledge and is always available at a price. This is the market end of this chain. The other end is the R&D stage where new knowledge is generated and is added to the existing knowledge. An RTO, being in the business of generation and dissemination of knowledge, is, by definition, located at the latter end of the knowledge chain. The market, therefore, does not govern an RTO; the market begins at the margin of RTO operations.

Being governed by the market, or, operating in the market, on the other hand, will mean that there is a given price for the services of the RTO, and an RTO is one among many offering such services. The client chooses the lowest-priced supply. This is the market of ready-to-use knowledge. This is, again, typically the diffusion end of a stock of knowledge, which is distinct from the generation of knowledge, the price of which is yet to be negotiated. In the context of technological innovations, Arrow (1962a) observed that while innovation in a marketplace would be minor in nature, institutional intervention was necessary for major innovations. Recall our discussion on state patronage of an R&D organization. What is the basis of creation and patronization of such an organization outside the boundary of the corporate sector? It is the notion of addressing technological questions that the normal market forces failed to answer.

Being away from the market, an RTO's transactions have to be coordinated by the organization. An RTO has to create its own enterprise-specific human and physical assets and use them through an internal organization so that it can retain its unique position in the knowledge chain. The RTO-specific physical and human resources have to be distinctly different to enable the RTO to offer services that others are unable to offer. The efficiency of the internal organization is, therefore, the key to the creation and the utilization of distinct human and physical resources.[12]

This is achieved through networks of organizational linkages. Much of the efficiency of an internal organization depends on the capability of an RTO to access information and address the problems of the prospective users of its services.

Operating in a network mode is actually a process of internalizing the future market of RTO capability. The market does not exist *ab initio*.

It has to be constituted with the prospective user of RTO capabilities and the knowledge base in mind. Again, being away from the market, there is no price mechanism that will bring an RTO closer to the users of its services. An RTO has to gain privileged access to financial, physical, and human assets, and also information through a widespread vertical and horizontal network of various other organizations. The organizations to be networked with will be drawn from the other two worlds (the world of the RTO's knowledge fraternity and the world of the users of its knowledge base). Industrial R&D, in this model, is a concurrent activity where the user and creator of new knowledge work in partnership with each other. This model is radically different from the classical understanding where research in the laboratory results in innovation through different stages of technology transfer. In a network-based partnership model, transfer of technology is an integral part of the research itself. Following Aiken and Hage (1968), such a network can be described as interdependence of organizations or organizational exchange. An organization sacrifices a part of its autonomy for gaining access to the resources of other organizations. Such interdependencies, in turn, change the 'internal organizational diversity' (Aiken and Hage 1968).

Another important dimension of organization has been brought out by Herbert Simon's theory of bounded rationality or the limited cognitive ability of individual human beings (Simon 1957). The theory suggests that individual human beings have limitations in accessing and processing information and converting it into knowledge and innovation. An enterprise as an organization actually facilitates itself with the benefit of a combined and cooperative effort in accessing and processing information for creating and accumulating knowledge. While an organization accesses information through its network, it has to have organizational arrangements for processing acquired information to knowledge. The process has to add value to accessed information, and it has to be fast enough to retain its value because the flow of information over a long period of time without any value addition loses its meaning. The process also has to ensure that the knowledge thus created and possessed by the individuals of the organization is utilized fully by the organization and is finally transformed into innovation (Choo 1996).

These three actions, however, are concurrent rather than sequential. They characterize an innovative or learning organization. It has been argued that 'the hallmark of tomorrow's most effective organizations will be their capacity to learn' (Adler and Cole 1993).

Basic principles, practices and performance indicators

Four basic principles guide a responsive RTO as an organization.

1. An RTO has to internalize its market. This will mean having privileged access to the information about the clients' needs, their future strategies, and resources. This means it has to build up a partnership with the users of its knowledge base, and also with its fraternity in the world of knowledge-generation. An RTO may have a strategy of building up a partnership with the users of its services. Appropriate practices are needed to make such a strategy work. The basic element of partnership is mutual trust. This trust is built up gradually through a process of inter-organizational interactions. Involvement of clients in the decision-making process, and the widest possible interpersonal interactions among the personnel of RTOs and their client organizations build up mutual trust and partnership. The practices of RTOs, therefore, have to be examined in terms of their potential to expand interpersonal interactions with client organizations.
2. RTOs have to work in a network mode. Although it is implied in (1) it needs to be emphasized that while functioning in a network mode, RTOs have to sacrifice their autonomy to the necessary extent. As Araoz (1994) observed, one of the major problems of ailing RTOs is the practice of working in isolation as an autonomous entity. The degree of autonomy retained or sacrificed by an RTO is an important qualitative indicator of best practices. Every practice, for this purpose, has to be examined to see if it insulates the RTO decision-making process from the external inputs.
3. There should be a smooth flow of accessed information across the organizational hierarchy in the minimum time and with value addition. The practices of RTOs have to be examined in terms of their contribution to information processing and value addition. This issue is also quite closely linked with the autonomous entity of the RTOs.
4. An RTO has to transform itself into an organization that has human resources at the core. Human resources is a dynamic concept. An organization will have a mandate, a set of purposes to fulfill and goals to achieve. The manpower enrolled by an organization has to be appropriately skilled to be transformed into human resources to be able to achieve these goals. In addition, RTOs have to continuously upgrade and update their human resources. The practices of an RTO also have to be examined to see how they influence its human resources, and how far this human-embodied knowledge is available to the organization.

Are these principles of any practical use for suggesting the best organizational practices of RTOs? Performance indicators have to serve two purposes in this regard. They have to be directly related to the clearly defined objectives of a particular process or sub-process. They also have to have the organizational principles mentioned earlier as intrinsic properties. Now we shall try to redefine a sub-process and construct performance indicators sub-process-wise to examine the best practices suggested for these processes.

An analysis of best practices

In Chapter 5, we selected a set of functionally related processes and sub-processes for an illustrative exercise of benchmarking the best practices. Here, we shall take them up one after another and examine the suggested best practices in the light of the objective behind a practice, and how close these practices are to the organizational principles. We shall also discuss the appropriateness and efficacy of performance indicators used in the WAITRO study and how other indicators can complement or supplement them.

Process: Service

Sub-process: Service mix

Objective.   Going back to the model in Chapter 4, the main objective behind a carefully chalked out service mix is to create necessary conditions for the creation and use of knowledge for industrial clients. An RTO has three main activities: basic research, applied research and common technical services. A proper mix of these activities is important because they are complementary to each other. To reiterate the argument in Chapter 4, basic research creates the knowledge foundation in the possession of an RTO. Applied research helps in the conversion of the knowledge base for application in the production system through development and transfer of technology. Common technical services provide technical aid to the regular and routine technical problems of the production system.

Performance indicators used in the WAITRO study.   Growth in revenue and evidence of active interaction with clients.

Best practice.   How can it be ascertained if an RTO has the right activity mix? The problem becomes more complex if the RTO is mandated to provide only one kind of service. Again, it is neither always wise nor desirable for an RTO to get involved in all types of activities. This may mean thinly spreading RTO resources in too many activities while doing nothing significant. The main point, however, in service mix is the complementarity among service types, where one type of activity provides knowledge input to other activities. Thus, activities related to basic research have to provide inputs to the other two services and vice versa. If an RTO is concentrating on only one type of activity, it also has to access complementary inputs of other services from other organizations. It cannot shut its eyes to other services.

In the WAITRO study, it was seen that RTOs providing comprehensive services to clients also had best performance in terms of revenue earning from the clients. They had done much better compared to the RTOs that concentrated fully on services for revenue-generation. In fact, it was observed that RTOs mandated to provide only routine technical services or RTOs that had gradually shifted towards routine services for the generation of more revenue (for the case of IRTs, see Chapter 7) were actually languishing for survival.

It has also been observed that for the RTOs in developing countries, where industries are not fully technologically oriented, a kind of technological nursing of the industrial clients is required. In the case of India, there are a variety of organizations like Regional Testing Centres, Small Industry Service Institutes, and District Industry Centres that provide specific routine services to industries. There are similar organizational set-ups in the other developing countries of Asia and Africa. The services that these organizations are supposed to provide are so compartmentalized that a client has to approach various agencies for different types of needs. Again, all these services are geared to provide support to the existing technological practices of the industry. For any new technological innovations, clients have to help themselves or approach some other organization located elsewhere. Shortage of capital and limited market power that characterize the small units in developing countries make such technological ventures almost impossible. Without infusion of new technology, there can be no growth in the client industries, and without growth in the client industries, the RTOs will remain perpetually dependent on financial aid from other sources (mainly the government in the case of developing countries). Such dependence finally means alienation of the RTO from its clients. Technology nursing, therefore, needs single-window comprehensive services to clients.

Compare this with the case of prefecture laboratories. Many of these laboratories have made a mark internationally in new technology development, and all of them are supposed to provide comprehensive services to their prefectural clients. All these laboratories again maintain strong networks with universities and other national laboratories for accessing resources for their clients. Many of them also have strong networks with financial institutions for enabling diffusion of new technological innovations.[13]

Another important aspect of technological nursing is the transfer of proven technology to the industries. This has been suggested as the most relevant activity for RTOs from the less developed countries of Africa and Asia. The transfer of proven technology indeed demands a comprehensive capability on the part of an RTO.

Observation on WAITRO indicators.   The service mix of an RTO evolves over the years. Evolution depends on the RTO's responsiveness to interaction with clients and its ability to articulate their needs. For monitoring the right service mix, revenue earned may be a guide in the sense that if service mix is appropriate, revenue is supposed to show an increasing trend. But the contrary, that is, revenue is increasing so the RTO has an appropriate service mix, may not hold. Revenue earning as an indicator, therefore, has to be complemented by qualitative indicators to examine if one activity is actually providing inputs to other activities. Such complementarity in activities can be established through an efficient internal communication system. We have dealt with this aspect later.

Sub-process: Determination of service mix to be offered

Objective.   It is important to have a practice in place that appropriately addresses the needs of the target client. The needs of the target client mean both present and future needs. For achieving this, the target client has to be defined carefully and precisely. Industry-specific RTOs have a much easier task in this regard, whereas it becomes complex for RTOs dealing with a variety of clients from different industrial segments. An example is RTOs engaged in specific technology areas like electronics with applications in many industries. In agricultural research, in the less developed countries, RTOs undertake research projects funded by various government agencies. The beneficiaries of such projects are common farmers. In such cases, a distinction has to be made between beneficiaries and clients. The farmers, in this particular case, will not be the clients; they will be the beneficiaries. The clients will be the agencies that would carry the new farming technology to the farmers.[14]

Clients are clearly identified when RTOs are engaged in a client-funded project. In fact, projectization of all RTO activities, general services as well as internally funded exploratory research activities, help in defining clients clearly. Once the clients have been identified, they have to be involved at every stage from project selection, its execution, and on to the transfer of knowledge. This is not a process of maximizing revenue from clients but a process identification of scope of technological intervention in clients' activities and also ensuring the process of new innovations. If clients are considered as the marketplace, this is also a process of internalization of the market as one of the basic organizational principles of RTO effectiveness highlighted earlier. The process of internalization also means giving up the autonomy of functioning and allowing space for outside inputs in the RTO decision-making process.

Performance indicators used in the WAITRO study.   Client satisfaction survey and growth in client revenue.

Best practice.   RTO activities have to be based on feedback from prospective clients. For receiving such feedback, RTOs have to build up extensive and intensive interactions with clients. The quality of such interactions in terms of the feedback received improves with more person-to-person interactions compared to impersonalized interactions like newsletter, brochure, seminar and so on. In fact, more emphasis on impersonalized interaction is one way of retaining autonomy.

It was observed in the WAITRO study that RTOs having a well-defined client group also have an organizational arrangement for interactions with clients. In such cases, clients are also in a position to articulate the service types and mix they would need. Organized arrangement for interaction, however, is the best practice, irrespective of the diverse or unique nature of clients. By organized arrangements we mean there are well-defined stages where clients would be involved in decision-making. For the RTOs of Asia and Africa, where technological competitiveness is not the prevalent industrial culture, the technology push and policy push kind of approach cannot be avoided. Most of these RTOs are dependent on funds from the government, which then wholly directs their activities. The role of clients in decision-making is truncated and passive. The case of the IRTs (see Chapter 7) can be cited here as an example of the passive role of clients.

Observation on WAITRO indicators.   The revenue earned from clients will indicate the RTO's performance in a quite roundabout way. If the process of determining the service is appropriate, clients will be happy, and, if clients are happy they will access RTO services with more regularity, and, therefore, RTO revenue will increase. The performance indicator for this process, on the other hand, has to be one that can suggest the extent of involvement of the clients in the process of project planning and execution by RTOs. At this stage, one may be tempted to develop quantitative measures of interactions in terms of how many types of interactions and with what regularity. The most effective way, however, is to examine the process of project selection and how much more room can be created for feedback from the users of the project output. It is possible to detail the stages of selection and the execution process of different projects, and examine at how many meaningful stages the identified clients are involved. The more the involvement the better would be the practice. The question that remains thereafter is one of how personalized and active is the involvement of the clients? By personalized involvement we mean whether, in the process of interaction, the clients are directly interacting with the RTO management and its core personnel, or is it a process where a client is one in the crowd and is not sure whether he is being heard? Clients are said to be actively involved if they are forthcoming with their views and arguments and see to it that their suggestions are considered. It was seen in the course of the WAITRO study that many RTOs had extensive involvement of clients in the decision-making process, but chose to keep such involvement as passive as possible. This is a subtle way to retain autonomy behind the facade of opening up.

Clearly, such indicators are not always quantitative. It is, however, not difficult to delineate the decision-making process of an RTO and to identify the scope of involvement of clients. Once the process is delineated, the nature of interaction is easily distinguishable (between personalized and impersonalized, and between active and passive involvement).

Sub-process: Ensuring service quality

Objective.   This is the ultimate means of building up RTO credibility with its clients. The practice of ensuring the quality of services is, therefore, one of the most critical organizational processes. The objective is not only to ensure the clients' need for quality, but also to make them aware of the continuous process of improvement and provide services to that end.

Performance indicators used in the WAITRO study.   Client satisfaction survey and growth in client revenue.

Best practice.   Like the earlier process, the quality of service can also be ensured through an organized interaction with the clients. And again, an impersonalized practice, like a client satisfaction survey, might create a distance between the client and the RTO. Such surveys might also bring in responses that would be subject to multiple interpretations. There are two sides to these practices for ensuring service quality. One is having the right information about the level of dissatisfaction and another is attending to quality problems. Organized interactions like regular visits to the clients' office, their participation in projects and so on are ways to get information about their level of satisfaction. In the WAITRO study, it was seen that in many RTOs, the processing of such information for appropriate actions was constrained by a strong departmentalization of RTO activities. An organized effort to attend to the complaints of clients, therefore, has to be accompanied by non-departmentalization of RTO activities.

Observation on WAITRO indicators.   In the WAITRO study, it was observed that RTOs with growing client revenue also had an organized arrangement of interaction in matters of quality. Some of them had quality certification under a recognized quality programme. Some of them even undertook a survey of satisfaction. As argued earlier, RTOs that provide quality services are expected to attract more and more clients, and, therefore, are also expected to have a growth in revenue. But, at the same time, growth in revenue may not always mean that there are no complaints about the quality of services. RTOs providing statutory technical services, or monopoly services that are highly subsidized (not dependent on clients' revenue) may find growth in revenue without being careful about quality. Getting certification under a recognized quality programme is definitely a good way of initiating clients into RTO services. But retaining clients and developing credibility will depend upon the subsequent experience of clients with the quality of RTO services.

Revenue-based indicators of the quality of RTO services, therefore, have to be strengthened by indicators of practices for accessing, processing and responding to clients' feedback. We have already pointed out the importance of personalized practices over impersonalized practices like a survey on the clients' satisfaction level. Some quantifiable indicators could be the number of complaints received from personal contacts between RTO personnel and clients, and the response time for attending to such complaints. A qualitative indicator would be an assessment of the information flow within the organization. We shall discuss the qualitative indicators for information flow later.

Process: Linkages and interaction with clients

Sub-process: Making RTO capability known, or awareness-creation strategy

Objective.   The objective here is to have practices that would project RTO services, capabilities, and successes to the clients and to those who would fund RTO activities. The distinction between the client and the funder is that while the former is a direct user of RTO services, the latter funds RTO activities for a targeted beneficiary. Funders could be national or local governments, or different national and international funding agencies.

Performance indicators used in the WAITRO study.   Growth in client revenue, cost of awareness-building over client revenue, percentage of client revenue, assessment of amount and quality of awareness activities.

Best practice.   In the WAITRO study, the practices under this heading are grouped according to the focus of the awareness-building activities. Such activities could be general in nature for all and sundry. They could be targeted at a particular company, a group of companies, funders, a particular region, or even at the international community of clients and funders. There are a few interesting dimensions that need to be brought out here. In terms of the cost of awareness-building and a growth in revenue from clients, RTOs focusing on major client groups do better. RTOs that have a particular territory to serve have a higher promotional cost and earn lower revenue. RTOs focusing on a particular industry segment do better with a lesser amount of promotional cost.

Brochures, advertisements, newsletters and so on are common practices for every type of client. These practices are expensive but unavoidable because they are formal releases that document RTO capability and successes. This is the material that clients carry back home with them as reference material after a more personalized exposure to RTO activities. Thus, the cost–revenue ratio of promotional activities will be more favourable if accompanied by activities like client-group-targeted seminars, workshops, company visits, inviting client personnel to the RTO, active participation in industry associations and so on that bring the RTO and the client face to face. For RTOs with a territorial focus (like the prefectural laboratories of Japan) it has been seen that the practice of 'free on-site consultancy' works wonders for building up the RTO's image for its clients. RTOs having a sizeable number of international clients actively nurture their relationship with local branches or subsidiaries.

One of the most successful among them even inducted representatives of MNCs in the governing board. Such direct interactions are complemented with hosting international meetings and seminars, and also encouraging publications in international journals.

In the case of RTOs that have to interact with technologically less mature industrial clients, there is no alternative to direct interactions between the RTO and the target client. In such cases, training programmes are most important and least-cost promotional activities of RTO capability and image building.

Promotional activities based on releases of formal documents of RTO capability and successes are expensive. Let us call them direct promotional activities. Another set of activities that bring RTOs and their clients face to face (like seminars, workshops, joint project planning, industry visits, training programmes, etc.) are indirect and least-cost promotional activities. Direct activities become much more effective only when they form a part of the indirect activities.

Observation on WAITRO indicators.   In the cost–revenue-based indicators only the cost of direct promotional activities is included. The cost of indirect activities is hidden and, therefore, cannot be estimated. Such indicators alone may overestimate or underestimate the impact of practice. Results derived on the basis of cost–revenue indicators have to be examined by the assessment of proportion of direct and indirect activities to ascertain that direct activities are only a part of indirect activities and indirect activities have clear priority.

Sub process: Identification of clients' needs

This sub-process has been examined separately for individual clients and for groups of clients. The nature of needs as well as the extent of RTO involvement both vary for individuals and groups of clients.

Identification of an individual client's needs

Objective.   An individual client's needs are related to the strategic planning of a particular firm in an industry. The strategic planning would generally address a new product, process, or pricing strategy to be derived from technological advantage. An RTO has to have the right practice to be able to generate confidence in such clients.

Performance indicators used in the WAITRO study.   Growth in client revenue and client interaction.

Best practice.   Reaching out to clients as opposed to the practice of waiting for the client is undoubtedly the best practice. RTOs adopt novel ways for gaining the confidence of clients. The WAITRO study has observed about 12 different practices adopted by RTOs. It has been found that RTOs having a better client revenue earning have as many as ten ways (out of the 12 listed) of interacting with clients. This indicates that a formal liaison office as a window for interaction with clients is not sufficient. Even common practices like representations of RTO personnel in the client's board or industry association, and vice versa alone cannot ensure a dynamic relation over a long period of time, because in most cases such representations turn out to be more decorative than active.

There are a few unique practices that RTOs can easily adopt to ensure a long-term relationship with clients. Let us take an example of an RTO that runs a regular technical course offering a graduate degree in collaboration with a university. The course itself is highly rated by the industry and university and popular among graduate students. Students trained under the course join the industry and the RTO maintains live contact with its ex-students through a very active alumni association. These students work as a lifeline for active contacts between the industry client and the RTO.

We have already talked about the practice of 'free on-site consultancy' by the prefecture laboratories of Japan. This practice builds up the clients' trust in the capability of the RTO, and thereby offers an opportunity for its personnel to build up a partnership in the technological strategies of the client. The case of V-process technology for sand moulding exemplifies the strength of the consultancy practice (Oshini 1993).

The essence of the best practices discussed in this section is again personalized contact with clients in as many ways and with as much intensity as possible. The market is constituted of potential clients. It is to be noted that the nature of such personalized contact would vary with the practice. While all the means of establishing personal contacts are good, the best practice is the one that helps to build up a partnership with the potential clients or market. This is the process of internalizing the market that is achieved by shedding an autonomous style of functioning, and getting access to information from the clients' door.

Observation on WAITRO indicators.   Prefecture laboratories provide free on-site consultancy; they are also not mandated to maximize their revenue from clients. Then, how can we call their particular practice the best practice if practices are evaluated in terms of growth in client revenue? It is still the best practice because it satisfies the organizational principles of the non-autonomous mode of operation, is the least-cost access to market information, and has earned the trust of the clients. The best way to measure the effectiveness of such practices is to examine the intensity of client interaction. Keeping the organizational principles in mind, qualitative and quantitative indicators can be developed by identifying practices that provide critical feedback information from the client and help in formulating RTO activities. The observation remains the same for RTOs that are mandated to increase revenue earning. By not making revenue earning the main indicator, we have reversed the process. RTOs now try to have privileged access to information from clients, formulate their activities accordingly, and earn revenue by attending to their clients' technological aspirations.

Identifying client group's needs

Objective.   Here, the objective is to have the right practice that will enable RTOs to identify the needs of a group of clients. The services to attend to such needs target a group of clients. By definition, such services are not proprietary. An RTO's credibility in providing such services may also lead to proprietary services to individual clients.

Performance indicators used in the WAITRO study.   Growth in services offered by RTO, growth in client revenue, and client interaction.

Best practice.   Identification of client needs by the management based on an input from RTO staff, board members and regular meetings with the industry has been suggested as the best practice. Having a representation of clients in the board that makes decisions about the client group's needs has a real potential for building up a long-term interest of clients in the RTO. In fact, RTOs in such a case become a part of the clients and vice versa.

Observation on WAITRO indicators.   If the clients' needs are attended to more carefully, the services of the RTO will be accessed more regularly, and if the services are priced, the RTO will see a rise in revenue earning. The critical issue, therefore, is an identification of the needs of the client. It has been observed that industry association managements are doing well in this regard, not only in terms of revenue earning, but also in terms of improving existing services and adding new services to address the future changes in the market structure and market condition. The basic feature of RTOs managed by industry associations is the involvement of industry association representatives in the RTO decision-making system for programme formulation. It is, therefore, not the revenue earning from services, but the client group's direct involvement in the RTO's programme formulation activities that provides a clue to the best practice.

Process: Information flow

Close interaction with clients has been emphasized as the key to the effectiveness of RTO services. The purpose of such interaction is to get access to information about the clients' technological priorities and aspirations. We have argued that such interactions build up much-needed mutual trust and also a partnership with clients. Trust and partnership together can resolve the problem of technology transfer from the laboratory to the production system.

Information thus obtained from the production system needs to be processed for both decision-making and knowledge-generation. Information acquired but not processed will otherwise create a situation of information overload. The processing of information from the production system will need access to further information from the knowledge world or the world of other technology providers (knowledge-generation system). This is the world that offers a stock of knowledge for further research on problems thrown up by the production system.

The information accessed is received by the organization of an RTO and processed for its activities. The information flow within an organization is for value-addition leading to decision-making and knowledge-generation. For the present purpose, we have examined the process of information flow in terms of networks within the organization of an RTO and with the outside world.

Sub-process: Practices for networking with other technology providers

Objective. The need here is to develop mutually beneficial relationships with other technology providers so that the RTO can complement its core competence with that of others and have access to the information on contemporary developments on the knowledge frontier.

Performance indicators used in the WAITRO study. Growth in client revenue, the RTO's financial performance, and assessment of the process used.

Best practice. Activities related to networking have been divided into low-cost and high-cost activities. It has been seen that most of the RTOs in developing countries face resource constraints in active networking activities that entail high costs. RTOs having a better financial performance also actively pursue quite a few high-cost networkings. Most of the high-cost activities involve international contacts. RTOs with resource constraints cannot always access such contacts.

The essence of networking is to be found in strategic planning and the human resource development initiative of an RTO. Networks become alive with contacts between personnel of different organizations. At the same time, networking cannot be left only to the individual initiatives of an RTO. An RTO, through a network, has to look for strategic gains for capabilities that will be embodied in its human resources. Many RTOs have practices that leave even the high-cost network activities to individual initiatives. In such cases, RTOs face the problem of networking without any direction or clear purpose, and thereby entail a high cost without any strategic gain. Another aspect of networks sans strategy is the loss of human resources when through networks there are individual gains and RTOs fail to convert the individual gain into organizational gain. This observation is also true for low-cost networking.

Irrespective of the cost associated, networking activities become most effective when they are used as tools for attaining strategic goals. For doing that, networking has to be an organizational initiative. Much of the knowledge gain from networking is actually human-embodied. Networking, therefore, has to be accompanied by arrangements for deriving full organizational benefit from a human-embodied knowledge base. This will be discussed separately in relation to best practices for human resource development.

Observation on WAITRO indicators.   The practices for networking, therefore, need to be assessed by input from networking in the present and planned future activities. It also needs to be assessed by the gain in human resource creation and utilization by the RTO. Quantification of such gains is not very easy. A qualitative assessment, however, is possible if it is known who will be the best network partner for accessing a particular information or knowledge that is valuable for the RTO's present and future aspirations.

Sub-process: Practices for networking with industry

Objective.   To develop mutually beneficial relationships with industrial clients.

Performance indicators used in the WAITRO study. Growth in client revenue, and assessment of interaction with clients through various platforms of networking.

Best practice. Various types of interactions result in networking, and successful networking strengthens further interaction. The distinction between interaction and networking is that the latter is structured interaction for mutual benefit. We have argued how more personalized interaction helps to make different processes more effective. In the case of networking, we have to look for the mode of interaction that will lead to successful networking. The essence of the best practice in the WAITRO study is that an active involvement of clients in RTO affairs and vice versa, creates conditions for networking with clients. Such an active involvement is made possible by inducting the client industry into RTO committees that plan the RTO's present and future programmes.

Observation on WAITRO indicators. It is possible to trace the types of interactions that lead to networking with clients. All the channels of interaction have to be assessed by the extent to which they involve clients in RTO affairs. Revenue earnings from the client are definitely not a direct indicator for assessing the efficiency of networking.

Sub-process: Practices for internal communication

Objective. Internal communication is a process in which information acquired from external sources is processed. From the point of accession, the information has to flow within the organization, along and across the hierarchy. An efficient system of internal communication instills an understanding of common purpose in the employees, and an appreciation of each other's role in the organization. The internal communication system of an organization becomes functional in two ways. The first is by ensuring interpersonal interaction and cooperation. This is ensured by the internal organizational structure and the responsibility/ authority granted at different levels. Let us call them active processes of internal communication. In this we have included sub-processes, like overall organizational management style, grouping of RTO capabilities, responsibility granted to organizational units and functional authority structure. We shall discuss these sub-processes separately. The second is the passive process. Such processes are media- and social-activity-based. However, for the purposes of this study we shall only deal with the active processes for internal communication.

Performance indicators used in the WAITRO study.   Financial performance, growth in client revenue, growth in staff or budget and an assessment of how well the clients' needs are met.

Best practices.   If we observe the best practices for all the sub-processes,
we shall notice that they differ from each other mainly in terms of
decentralization of responsibility and authority, and also scope of interpersonal interaction and cooperation. There is a connection between
the financial performance of RTOs and the extent of decentralization
and scope of interaction and cooperation. We can also draw a similar
conclusion by examining these practices in terms of the organizational
principles mentioned earlier.

Thus, in the overall organizational management style, practice (c)
(see Annexure) is the best practice because, when compared with other
hierarchical and centralized systems of information processing and
decision-making, this practice makes RTO activities more focused,
participative, and rewarding.

Similarly, technology-based grouping of RTO capability creates a scope
for accessing knowledge from different sources for addressing a technological problem. It also ensures interaction and collaboration among
experts. Exchange of knowledge and cooperation enhance the scope for
knowledge expansion. Such groupings of RTO capabilities along with
group-level responsibility for delivering the output and also functional
authority for project team creation and project management within
time and budget would create a condition for a learning organization.

Observation on WAITRO indicators.   It has been observed that RTOs with
a more decentralized authority structure, and participative management
show better financial performance. However, we shall argue that the
essence of better performance is organizational efficiency achieved by
having the practices of a learning organization.

Process: Human resources

Sub-process: Attracting the best manpower and retaining it

Objective.   It is important to have the right practice that will ensure
that RTOs have the right manpower. The dilemma here is between
recruiting the best personnel and recruiting the potential manpower to
train them according to the needs of the organization. Both the practices have their corresponding advantages and disadvantages. Getting
trained manpower with proven capability helps to minimize the cost of

manpower development. At the same time, human resources created within the organization would be far more loyal to the organization than manpower trained in other organizations. Besides, the manpower trained within the organization will be more familiar with the organizational culture and work ethics. However, in the case of organizational restructuring, such manpower may become a disadvantage. The most important issue related to human resources is the creation of organization-specific resources that contribute to organizational learning. Another point that needs to be kept in mind while recruiting manpower is the aging of an organization. The experience and tacit knowledge that an organization develops over the years should help it to have a right mix with the new and fresh flow of manpower. The new entrants will get the benefit of working with experienced hands, and they will also bring fresh life and initiatives to the organization.

Performance indicators used in the WAITRO study.　Assessment of satisfaction with present process, growth in client revenue, growth in staff, and personnel hired in a year.

Best practice.　Most of the prefecture laboratories of Japan prefer to recruit fresh people at the entry points, and train them in a way so that they are useful to the organization. The RTOs of the developing countries of Asia and Africa recruit new personnel at the entry point as well as experts at higher levels. In the government-promoted RTOs in these countries, including Japan, recruitment rules are quite rigid and long-winded. In many RTOs of developed countries there are more flexible processes that use input from managers, co-workers and human resource experts to select new personnel. It has been observed that RTOs that are more financially independent enjoy more flexibility in recruiting their own personnel. On the other hand, RTOs dependent on government grants have to go through various types of approvals from different government departments. They also have to follow various rules and regulations attached to grants from the government exchequer. Many RTOs have found ways to get around the rigid regulations by hiring personnel on a contract basis, instead of on a regular basis. Such contracts are generally for personnel at the entry point level. Contract personnel with potential, in many cases, are then given regular appointments. This serves two purposes. On the one hand, RTOs are able to avoid the rigid rules that constrain recruitment of fresh manpower; on the other hand, a reservoir of contract personnel comes in handy, should there be any recruitment in the future. The organization, however, loses if it fails to make the best use of the manpower it has trained.

The flexibility enjoyed by an RTO in recruiting its own manpower is also related to the nature of the manpower market. RTOs in developed countries compete in the manpower market with many other employment opportunities offering various types of alternative career options. If the recruitment rules are not flexible enough, and opportunities offered are not competitive enough, RTOs would lose out on the best manpower in the market. However, RTOs in developing countries have limited career opportunities to offer. Such RTOs will have a stock of manpower seeking entry into the organization. Attracting or retaining manpower, therefore, is not a major problem for the organization. Nevertheless, such RTOs generally suffer from the inertia of a monopolist. They show a tendency to take their manpower for granted and offer very few internal mechanisms for human resource development.

In the case of IRTs, manpower is recruited at the entry point and trained over the years by the RTO only to lose them to client industries where career opportunities are better. The clients get trained manpower without incurring any additional costs (see Chapter 7).

Flexibility in recruiting manpower, no doubt, is a pre-condition for adopting a best practice. However, such flexibility exists and can be exercised only if RTOs have substantial financial independence. Financial independence in turn implies enough revenue generation by RTOs through regular activities. Here, the question of service mix acquires a new dimension. We shall argue that financial independence of an RTO does not necessarily mean activities for revenue maximization. It is possible though to acquire the necessary financial independence by disseminating the existing stock of knowledge or knowledge at various stages of maturity to prospective users and also to the RTO fraternity. Such acts of dissemination of knowledge may take the form of training, seminars, consultancy and so on.

Observation on WAITRO indicators.   The quantitative indicators used in the WAITRO study are again broad macro-level indicators. To arrive at process-specific indicators we have to supplement these indicators with a set of related questions. These questions are as follows:

1. Have the activities of the RTO, over the years, moved to the frontiers of its research areas, or, in other words, have its capabilities enhanced over the years for handling more knowledge-intensive projects?
2. Are RTO activities impeded because of a lack of appropriate manpower?

3. Does the RTO have enough flexibility in taking decisions regarding recruitment?
4. Is the flexibility being impeded because of financial dependence?
5. Has the RTO explored all the possibilities of revenue-generation through the dissemination of its stock of knowledge?

Sub-process: Practices for capability-building

Objective. The difference between manpower and human resources is that the former is transformed into the latter by inducing the right skill tuned to the long-term needs of the organization. This transformation is an ongoing and continuous process because otherwise today's resources may become obsolete tomorrow. From the employees' point of view too, an organization becomes an attractive place to work in if it offers opportunities for acquiring new skills on the job or through training in other institutions.

The practices for capability-building, therefore, have to address the question of priority areas, incentives and ensure that the skills of its employees are used appropriately. If one side of capability-building is identification of the areas that need strengthening, the other side is to have the right arrangements and opportunities for the employees to access various capability-development programmes. The question of how areas of capability-building are identified by an RTO is, therefore, coupled with what the RTO does to build capability.

Performance indicators used in the WAITRO study. Client satisfaction survey, staff satisfaction survey, overall RTO performance, percentage of budget spent for offering capability-building opportunities, and the number of new service areas initiated.

Best practice. A wide variety of practices have been identified by the WAITRO study. RTOs in Asian countries mainly adopt internal mechanisms either through the governing body of the RTO or the RTO chief (sometimes with the help of external experts, or in consultation with the divisional heads) to identify the areas of capability-building. In the case of RTOs in North America, it is the individual scientists who are expected to identify opportunities and submit their proposal to the management for decisions. In many cases, proposals from individual scientists are supplemented by inputs from external and internal committees. On the other hand, the European RTOs use a combination of sources (board, external committees, management and employees) as inputs for the management to take decisions on capability-building activities. African RTOs are somewhat different from the rest. Most of them are dependent on donors' programmes for capability-building, so their own practices are only rudimentary.

As a principle, the practice that is governed by inputs from clients and other external sources that have stakes in RTO achievements would be the best practice. Therefore, it is not a good practice if the RTO chief alone takes decisions about the needs and scope of capability-building. On the other hand, the governing body of an RTO, which is constituted of representatives of clients and other peers and is actively involved in the activities of the RTO, is likely to be a good guide for capability-building programmes. Ideally, the long-term strategy of the RTO and identification of the areas of capability-building have to go hand in hand. The RTO management (and/or governing body) that is fully informed and involved in the process of making a long-term strategy for the RTO would be in the best position to articulate the needs of capability-building. Inputs from external experts, clients and internal staff enrich the decision and make it more acceptable.

Once the areas of capability-building are identified, an adequate incentive has to be there to motivate the staff to upgrade their skills and also make use of the upgraded skills for the benefit of the RTO. RTOs follow a combination of various methods for building the capabilities of their staff. Major practices, in this regard, identified in the WAITRO study, can be distinguished by the following three broad characteristics.

1. Staff-driven and ad-hoc initiatives.
2. A formal system for capability-building (acquiring higher degrees, regular arrangements with external agencies and institutions for training staffs in emerging areas, etc.).
3. Capability-building practices that are integrated in research projects (including core grant projects and also client-funded projects to develop certain skills).

It would be best to use a combination of these practices. However, much depends on the availability of resources to fund various programmes for skill development. Most RTOs feel that the best way of capability-development is to undertake research projects in new areas (either by using internal resources or client-funded projects). This works almost like on-the-job training for the staff. Again, skills thus developed being specific to the long-term strategy of the organization, making best use of the upgraded capability is easier. Such advantages are not available when the staff undertake skill development programmes on their own initiative. Such programmes may not be tuned to the strategic plans of the RTOs.

Observation on WAITRO indicators.   In the WAITRO study, it was observed that RTOs less dependent on grants from the government and other sources, and substantial revenue earnings from clients, have capability-building practices that are based on inputs from various stakeholders. Financial independence works in two different ways. First, the RTO does not have to be governed by the stipulations of the agency giving the grant. Secondly, an RTO has to retain its independence by continuously upgrading its capabilities. Hence, an RTO has to be evaluated by the skill that it possesses compared to the state-of-the-art skill level in its field.

Sub-process: Practices for career opportunities

Objective.   Career opportunities to the staff need to be seen as incentives for retaining staff in the RTO. The question of retaining comes when staffs with a particular capability are considered useful for the knowledge stock of the RTO. Career opportunities, therefore, are closely linked with the strategies of the RTO for capability-building. Career opportunities are also an integral part of the opportunity for capability-building for the individual staff. An organization that provides attractive opportunities for capability-building in emerging areas also attracts the best manpower. In fact, the practices for career opportunities in an RTO have to be appropriate for attracting and retaining the best manpower.

Performance indicators used in the WAITRO study.   Overall RTO performance, and assessment of satisfaction with the present practice.

Best practice.   Career opportunities are associated with evaluation systems. It has been observed that there are two broad evaluation systems. One is based solely on the performance management system, and the other is performance evaluation with a stipulated period of residency at a particular level. Performance assessment is made in a variety of ways. It is generally based on productivity or the output of an employee. This needs a clear understanding of the output expected from an employee. Even if output can be clearly defined, it may not be easy to estimate an individual's contribution in a team or group activity. In many RTOs, assessing the money value of the business brought in or the worth of the business accomplished by an employee simplifies the problem. Such a system has an in-built revenue-maximization bias. We have already discussed the shortcomings of the revenue-maximization approach. In many cases, evaluation is based on the RTO chief's assessment of the performance of an individual. In the RTOs of many developing countries there is an elaborate system of performance management that incorporates internal, external and experts' assessment of an employee's contribution over a stipulated period of time. Such a system would entail a huge administrative cost and delay in the process of appropriately rewarding the employees.

Basing advancement from one technical/professional level to another on the results of the performance evaluation by the management system is considered the best practice in the context of North American RTOs. In the Asian subcontinent, it is interesting to observe that in 13 of the 20 RTOs under study, there was no promotional reward for the employees. Although the practice of *in situ* promotion might provide great material incentive to employees, it closes the door for external competition at the risk of heavy inbreeding. One RTO has a unique practice – a percentage of vacant positions are kept for internal promotion and the rest are open for external competition. This practice helps in getting new people and at the same time gives opportunity to the existing staff to compete through their performance.

Observation on WAITRO indicators. Overall performance in terms of an RTO's human resources could be a guide to the best practices of providing career opportunity. It can also be gauged from the ability of the RTO to retain the best manpower. Consider the example of IRTs. They were steadily losing their best manpower to client industries. Our study could detect three reasons for this. The client industries laid unambiguous emphasis on opportunities for new skill development; there was more authority; and a better compensation package.

It was also observed that RTOs dependent on government funding broadly follow the practices of government departments for providing career opportunities to their employees. Since RTOs need different dynamics, work culture and ethos from a government department, following government practices indeed paralyses RTO activities.

Rounding off

In this chapter, our discussion focused on performance indicators for comparisons of practices. Performance indicators are the centre of gravity of any benchmarking exercise where the success of the exercise rests on its ability to make a distinction among practices. We were looking for performance indicators that could best identify the best practices for the selected processes and sub-processes of an RTO. We developed our discussion with reference to the WAITRO study. Some of the inferences from the above discussion can be summarized as follows.

Precautions for construction of PIs

1. We hypothesized a functional relationship between a process and its performance indicators. We also assumed such relations to be continuous and differentiable. In reality, organizational processes are not so. As a result, it may not be always possible to come to a precise conclusion on the basis of quantified performance indicators.
2. An organizational process functions in association with many other processes and practices. It may not be possible to single out the contribution of a particular process.
3. Many processes and practices could be passive and decorative. A macro-level performance indicator may overestimate the contribution of such processes.
4. An RTO is not a revenue-maximizing organization. Balance-sheet-based performance indicators, therefore, may be misleading.

Thus, we attempted to supplement broad macro-level performance indicators with sub-process-wise indicators. We also argued that quantitative indicators, although preferable, might not be always available when we are dealing with organizational practices. Qualitative indicators may be of great help in such situations. We suggested four basic organizational principles of an RTO as a guide for developing qualitative indicators. With examples from the WAITRO study, we showed how qualitative indicators could be used for sharpening our understanding of the best practices.

Qualitative versus quantitative indicators

The most remarkable aspect of qualitative indicators is that they can help to set the cause-and-effect relationship among the functional processes in the right perspective. To clarify the point let us take the example of the process called service mix and revenue earned by an RTO as an indicator of the appropriateness of the service mix. Let us recall that indicators are constructed from a perception of the functional relations between a process and its outcome. If the service mix is appropriate, more clients will access the service and therefore the RTO will earn more revenue. Earlier, we argued that the reverse of the relation might not be true. An RTO earning a higher revenue may very well mean a service mix that is more physical-asset-based than human-resource-based. As suggested earlier, such a situation may imply dwindling capabilities of the RTO. A revenue-based quantitative indicator, therefore, has to be evaluated by the appropriate qualitative indicator to verify the actual worth of the service mix. What we, therefore, suggest is that even in cases where quantitative indicators are easily available, a set of qualitative indicators would actually ensure the efficacy of the quantitative indicators.

Predetermined set of PIs

It follows that if we begin a benchmarking exercise of an RTO with pre-determined performance indicators, we may miss the actual issue affect-ing the performance of the RTO. Let us take the example of project approval in the IRA. The case is discussed in detail in the next chapter. The IRA wants to address the question of delay in project approval. If we study the practices of project approval prevailing in different RTOs, including the IRA, and we compare their performance in terms of the revenue earned, it may turn out that the IRA's practices are the best since it has a high revenue earning compared to other RTOs.

Note that in this example we have not addressed the question of delay in project approval directly. This was because we began with the given performance indicator and restricted our exercise to comparison in terms of that given indicator. Now let us begin with a situation where we do not have any given performance indicator. We study the approval procedure and stages involved in detail and compare them with the practices of other RTOs. We examine the practices in terms of the time taken, the number of steps needed, the different sources of information accessed, and the extent of the clients' involvement. The indicator has to reflect the efficiency of a practice in minimizing the time and maxi-mizing the inputs from external and internal sources. Such indicators have nothing to do with the revenue earning of an RTO. They can also not be predetermined, and can be constructed only after detailing the processes and practices.

What do we benchmark?

In the analysis of the practices in the process 'Determination of service mix', we suggested that clients should be treated as partners and not as beneficiaries. Partnerships with clients are built up through interactions. Such interactions help to derive valuable inputs from clients in terms of their needs and problems. The knowledge base thus developed helps to fine-tune the RTO service mix. We also argued that such interactions have to encourage person-to-person contact between the personnel of the RTO and the clients. We described 'free on-site consultancy' as a practice that helps to build up such interactions and in turn trust between the RTO and its prospective clients. While encouraging such interactions in an organized fashion, the RTO is actually breaking its own autonomy and accessing the benefit of the knowledge pool outside the boundary of the RTO.

What we focused on is that for the determination of the service mix of an RTO it is essential to have inputs from the users of the services of the RTO. Such inputs can be usefully accessed if the RTO has an organized arrangement for interpersonal interactions with its clients. This is what a process or a practice in a process has to do. In other words, this is the essence of a practice. There has to be a logistic arrangement for realization of the essence. The practice of 'free on-site consultancy' is one such logistic that ensures the essence of the practice for the determination of service mix. The logistics of a practice evolves over time through the trial-and-error process. The work ethos and the environment of an organization also influence the logistics of a practice. The organization, therefore, has to be vigilant on the logistic arrangements of a practice to ensure that it contains the essence of the practice.

What we benchmark is not the logistics arrangement of a practice, but the essence of a practice. This can be achieved only when the organization is continuously vigilant comparing logistics against essence.

7
Benchmarking in Practice

The WAITRO study was methodologically complex because the practices of 60 RTOs were being compared with each other. All the practices for a sub-process were grouped together on the basis of their essential similarities. It would have been much easier if the exercise had been done for a particular RTO with a clear idea of what was to be benchmarked. In the case of the WAITRO study, all the 60 RTOs would have their own specific characteristics. The practices had to be compared and the best practices had to be benchmarked, therefore, on an abstract level with a common denominator for all the RTOs. The effectiveness of RTO services for clients was chosen as a common denominator in the WAITRO study.

As a part of the WAITRO study, a second phase was designed for the actual benchmarking exercise of selected and willing RTOs. This phase had the twin purpose of sharpening the methodology and also of testing the feasibility of the benchmarking exercise. We studied two such cases in detail. As we shall see, in both the cases, the benchmarking exercise was done for a specific purpose and for a specific organizational problem. Both the studies were taken up with the full concurrence of the RTOs. The study team, therefore, had complete access to organizational information, some of it confidential. That is why, we had to change the name of the RTOs studied.

The first case was that of an RTO engaged in agricultural research. Let us call it the Institute of Research in Agriculture (IRA) where the management was concerned about the delay in decision-making. After an initial discussion, it was agreed that the main focus of the exercise would be information management. The second case was a group of textile research institutes managed by industry associations. Let us call it the Institute of Research in Textiles (IRT).

Information management in IRA[15]

Any organization can be seen as a structured arrangement for the flow of information up and down the hierarchy. Hierarchy again is an arrangement for information processing for the purpose of decision-making through knowledge-generation. The single most important act performed by an organization is to take advantage of the pool of knowledge as opposed to the problem of 'bounded rationality of individual knowledge'. But, a pool of knowledge is not the knowledge of just a few individuals put together. It needs to be ensured that the relevant individuals have access to the right information and they have the capability to process the same information. In other words, as the right information flows up and down the organizational hierarchy, it has to be enriched with value addition through information processing.

In the pre-liberalization and -globalization era, the types of information and value addition needed were different from the requirements of the new situation. As mentioned earlier, an important characteristic of the post-liberalization metamorphosis is that the IRA has to be quicker in decision-making and knowledge-generation than any other organization. A new-look IRA, therefore, has to be more efficient in processing the information flow.

Thus, the case study examines the information management system in the IRA to track the flow of information up and down the organizational hierarchy. The information flow has been examined in terms of the response time for the identification of the research problem and users' needs to outline the possible direction of changes.

Methodology

The methodology adopted is based mainly on mapping the information flow within the organizational structure of the IRA. As a first step, a broad organizational structure has been created. The broad structure has been broken down to bring into clear focus the critical areas of IRA activities that were specifically studied. These activities are:

1. approval of research projects;
2. evaluation and monitoring of R&D activities; and
3. output and services provided by the IRA.

The organizational structure of these activities has been superimposed on the information flow to understand the dimension of the flow and also the bottlenecks.

The value addition along the line of information flow has been gathered by extensively interviewing the heads of the research divisions and administration wings of the IRA. Note that the flow of information is neither documented, nor is it visible in any other form. To trace this flow down the line needs an a priori idea of the functional structure of the organization and its centre of gravity. The information flow, therefore, has to be constructed out of the functional structure of the IRA and points of value additions identified along the flow.

Approval of research proposal

We begin with an overall idea of sources of information commonly accessed by IRA personnel. Table 7.1 shows the information collected by the study team after talking to a wide cross-section of the staffs of IRA.

It is interesting to note that 90 per cent of the source of information is either the person himself or printed literature available in the library. For IRA, it is not that the globe is not accessible, but it appears that the organization wants to restrict its world. Internal communication, workshops, seminars and so on have no role to play as sources of information. The users of knowledge do not figure anywhere.

It is clear that information flow in such a situation is not required for value addition but only for approval or sanction from a higher authority. It is likely that such an organization is highly bureaucratic where information is of no value for knowledge-generation. In fact, the organization does not need any knowledge because it does not believe in the cognitive limitation of human beings. Extend this argument a little further to suggest that the organization of IRA is not required if we go by the definition of organization, which is to create a pool of human resources and use them in synergy. Referring to our discussion in earlier chapters we can describe the IRA as an RTO that operates in an autonomous mode. It fits well into the first ailments of the RTOs listed by Araoz (1994).

Table 7.1   Information channels used by IRA personnel

Channels	% of usage of channels
Personal knowledge, experience and experimentation	50
Personal or in-house library facilities and library personnel	40
Other personnel in organization, courses, workshops, etc.	8
Other channels	2

This being the broad nature of accessing information let us examine the internal information flow in IRA for the selected activities mentioned above.

Acquiring the information or idea from the channels mentioned above, the scientists of IRA transform it into a research matter. The lifeline passes from its origin to its approval as shown in Figure 7.1.

The principal scientist is one who formulates the research proposal. Research proposals are presented in the meeting of the RBC. The RBC holds a meeting at the divisional level with the principal scientist, the head of the division and other scientists. The structure of the RBC is shown in Figure 7.2(a).

The RBC has an interesting structure. The divisional head is the chairman of the RBC. In addition to faculty representatives, students are also represented. This is the first-level screening of the research proposal. This is again the only forum where the research content of proposals is discussed. For the students it is essentially a learning experience. Note that there is no representation from any outside agencies or prospective users in any meeting of the RBC.

This is important because, as we shall observe later, there is no other forum where the research content of any proposal is discussed. Being totally internal, the RBC finally turns out to be the legitimizing body for the IRA research activities, mainly as the first level of approval.

From the RBC a research proposal is sent to JD (Research) for approval through Research Proposal Form (I). JD (Research) actually works as a basket of research proposals to be taken up by the PIU. This unit scrutinizes this proposal through the Research Council (RC). The PIU is the central point of information flow. It is from this unit that the proposal

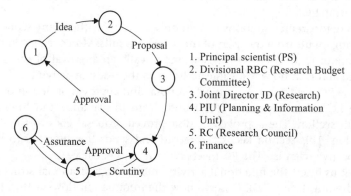

Figure 7.1   Flow of information for approval of internally funded research proposal

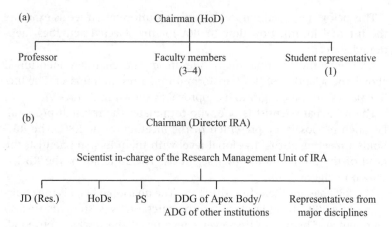

Figure 7.2   (a) The structure of the RBC; (b) the structure of the RC

goes to the RC for scrutiny. The RC is the most powerful body in the process of approval of any project proposed by scientists.

The structure of the RC is shown in Figure 7.2(b). Note that the RC has representations of JD (Research), Head of Departments (HoDs), and the Principal Scientist (PS), or the owner of the proposal. By this time, the proposal has already passed through all these stages before reaching the RC. The PS is the originator of the proposal. The HoD has approved it at the RBC level before it could reach the JD (Research). And after the JD (Research)'s consent it was sent to the RC through PIU. Only new representations in the RC are from the Deputy Director Generals (DDGs) and Additional Director Generals (ADGs) or from a higher level of hierarchy.

Here too, representations remain only in-house without any scope of getting inputs from the users of the research results. Moreover, given the nature of representations, it is again basically an approval of the proposal and is in no way a value addition to the research activities.

The RC scrutinizes the project proposal and approves or disapproves. The RC takes the assurance of funds from the Finance and Internal Audit section. The approved or disapproved proposal goes to the PIU section. This section keeps the record and sends the approval to the respective scientist. The RC meets twice in a calendar year.

Let us insert the functional activity into the organizational structure of the IRA (Figure 7.3). Observe how the information flows within the system.

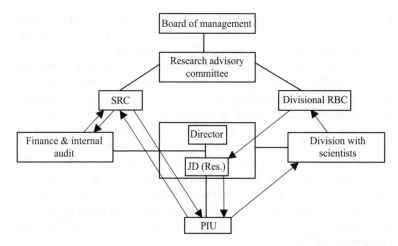

Figure 7.3   Information flow for approval of research proposal in different units of IRA

Figure 7.3 shows that the research proposal originates from the division and the information flows upward, for its approval, to the Divisional RBC and then to the JD (Research). It comes back to the scientist through the PIU after being scrutinized by the RC with approval or disapproval. What it brings out clearly is that the organizational structure, which is otherwise disintegrated, has been linked through forged channels of information flow. The long-winded flow of information is the result of the disintegrated nature of the organizational structure. By disintegrated structure we mean that the different components of the organization are not functionally related. These components might have originated for historical reasons and allowed to continue. They may have been accommodated in the system through complex and unnecessary channels of information flow.

The key issue here, however, is that most of the research proposals or functions are very inward-looking. They move around the concept of approval or disapproval. The scientist does not receive any value-added feedback. So at the end it does not concern the end-users. The main concern is the approval of the research proposal and sanction of the fund. This way there is no further value addition to most of the research results and the research loses its attraction midway. The net result is wastage of time as well as funds.

The problem associated with this style of functioning is the time lag between the origin of the research proposal and the approval of the proposal. Sometimes it takes a year for the approval to come through. In many cases, the proposal loses its importance or the researcher loses interest in the project over a long period of waiting.

The complex nature of information flow can be made simple. From the RBC to the RC, the route through JD and PIU is unnecessary. JD is anyway represented in RC and the PIU's job is to store the information. The act of storing information has been integrated with the act of information flow. The alternative route can be a short cut from the RBC to a reconstituted RC where, in addition to the existing representations, finance can also be involved. The PIU can be sent information for storage once the approval is finalized. The most important gain in this route will be in terms of time without curtailing the role of any authority.

For an externally funded project, the rules and regulations are a little less complicated. The flow of information for externally funded projects is shown in Figure 7.4.

Here, the outside funding agency with the collaboration of the respective division originates a research proposal. It passes through RBC to reach PIU. The proposal is signed by the JD (Research) and the Director and goes back to the PIU again. The PIU takes the assurance of funds from finance and internal audit and information about approval reaches the respective division, which informs the funding agency about the approval. If we merge the functional activity within the organizational structure we can observe the complex flow of information from one unit to another.

The main difference between an internally funded project and an externally funded project is that the latter takes less time to be approved than the former. The process in this case is less time-consuming not

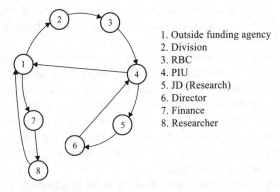

1. Outside funding agency
2. Division
3. RBC
4. PIU
5. JD (Research)
6. Director
7. Finance
8. Researcher

Figure 7.4 Information flow for the approval of an externally funded project

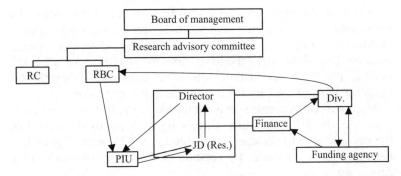

Figure 7.5 Information flow for an externally funded project within the organizational structure

because the procedure followed is simpler. The IRA, like any other research organization funded by the government, is under pressure to increase its external cash flow. As a result, not many questions are asked in the case of externally funded projects. The long and complex procedure otherwise remains the same in both internally and externally funded projects.

From Figure 7.5, we can observe that for the externally funded project, the rules and regulations are no different from those for the internally funded project. It also passes through a long chain where it gets delayed. There is a great difference in motivation for the scientists who have initiated an externally funded project. Externally funded projects ease the financial position of the division by having access to some extra-budgetary resources. Thus, not only the division, but the JD (Research) and the Director also become interested in externally funded projects.

Evaluation/monitoring

Once a research proposal is sanctioned, the research work starts in the respective divisions. After half a year, the principal scientist submits RPF (II) with information about the progress of the project work and an annual progress report by RPF (III). The RC is the monitoring as well as the evaluating agency for the research work actually done by the division or the scientists. The RC meets every six months or annually and reviews the programme. Sometimes the JD (Research) or the Director, along with the in-charge PIU, monitors activities through organized field/laboratory visits, discussion with principal scientists, and a review of the implementation through seminars and group meetings with scientific staff to find out the bottlenecks in the operationalization of the programme.

Ultimately, the report goes to the apex body through the Director. The information flow is shown in Figure 7.6. It shows the one-way upward information flow, which starts from the division where the research work has been done. Then the report goes to the PIU, which sends the same to the RC for evaluation. After scrutinizing the report, the RC sends the same to the Director and finally to the apex body.

When a report is prepared it is submitted to the PIU and from there it goes to the RC for scrutiny. Once a report is prepared, in most of the cases, it goes to the apex body through the Director (Figure 7.7). Rarely does any value-added suggestion or discussion flow back to the concerned scientist.

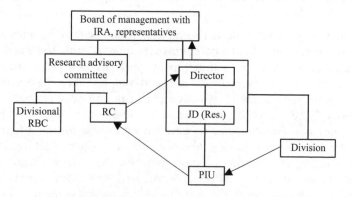

Figure 7.6 Information flow within the organization for the evaluation of an internally funded project

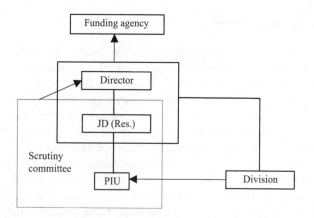

Figure 7.7 Information flow for the evaluation of an externally funded project

For externally funded projects, a separate scrutiny committee is constituted to monitor the research work. The committee comprises of JD (Research), Principal Investigator (PI), PIU in-charge and one or two referees, who, after scrutiny, send the report to the Director and finally to the funding agency. Project completion reports are submitted half-yearly or annually to the funding agency.

Forms of output and services

The following products and services are either generated as the outcome of research activities or provided as services on a regular basis to prospective users.

1. Products
   - Seed
   - Plant
   - Fertilizer
   - Machinery
2. Training
3. Consultancy
4. Testing

We had earlier examined the organizational arrangements that enable products and services to reach the users. Now we shall elaborate on the information flow in the activities related to the sale of seeds.

Sale of seeds

The target clients for seeds are farmers. They collect it from the IRA seed production unit. The information flows in the manner shown in Figure 7.8.

Divisions produce seeds of different varieties and send their products to the seed multiplication unit, where the seeds are multiplied and sent to the seed production unit. This unit has a sales counter for farmers. The sale proceeds go to the IRA central fund. If we put this functional activity into the organization structure we can observe the flow of information within the organization (Figure 7.9).

The production and multiplication units are separate and located outside the division under the control of a Joint Director (Research). The problem associated with this process is that there is no feedback process in the system. The function and liability of a division (that has

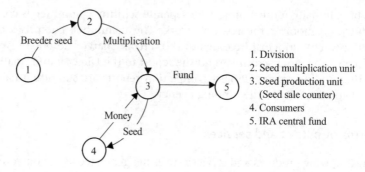

Figure 7.8 Information flow for the sale of seeds

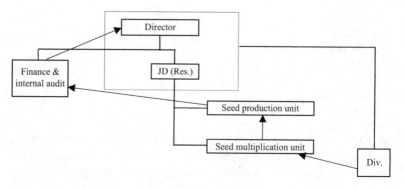

Figure 7.9 Information flow for the sale of seeds within the organization

developed the seeds) ends after handing the seeds over to the multiplication unit. The division and its researchers do not get any benefit of the revenue earned, nor are they involved in any kind of interaction with the users. The seed multiplication unit receives new seed varieties from different divisions. The multiplication division has limited land for multiplication and can multiply only a limited quantity of a particular variety. The IRA, therefore, can satisfy only a small number of users.

This sale of new seed varieties to farmers is called commercialization of IRA knowledge. Is it the sale of seeds or the sale of know-how that should be the point of interface for commercialization? This is the question that relates to the boundary of an RTO. We have already discussed this question in detail in the chapter on the effectiveness of R&D. It was argued there that an RTO would become more effective by restricting its activities around strategically defined core competence. Thus, if a textile research institute develops a new loom, the institute does not get into the production of the loom or weaving fabric in the new loom. In the specific case of the IRA, this means commercialization of its research know-how on a new seed variety and not production and sale of the new varieties.

This kind of spread of activities of an RTO is organizationally untenable too. Developing a new seed variety involves extensive research activities, whereas marketing and popularizing a new seed variety needs extensive marketing skills. In the case of agriculture, in addition, the farmers need to be convinced through demonstration and extension activities. Also, there has to be a proper infrastructure for the multiplication of the new seeds to meet the market demand. Integrating all these activities under a single organization would create an organizational juggernaut that would affect efficiency at every level.

The IRA, therefore, has to carefully define its clients. It has to have an interface with the farmers. Also, it has to have appropriate interactions with the breeders and seed farms – the clients for its research know-how. On the other hand, IRA scientists and researchers may directly interact with the already existing wide network for training their personnel on new seeds. This network will work as an interface for inputs from the IRA for demonstration and popularization of products based on IRA know-how.

Critical observations

We have looked into three critical areas of IRA research activities, namely, project selection and approval, evaluation and monitoring, and output and services provided by the IRA.

We began with the overall map of the organizational structure. This structure has been broken down into components to sift out the activity-specific organizational structure. We have superimposed the flow of information on the cross-section of the organizational structure to examine the mismatch and bottlenecks in the information flow.

It appears that the organizational structure of the IRA and the accompanying direction of information flow are predominantly oriented for decision-making – the traditional role of organization and information. In fact, the structure is more suitable for approval than taking decisions. The difference is to be understood in the sense that approval is subsequent to decisions that are expressed in terms of a certain set of rules. The decision-making in the aspects discussed here is on whether a proposed action or activity falls within this set of rules. This set of rules is generally rigid and the information flow we have discussed in no way provides feedback on the need for new rules. These rules are again subject to interpretation by the approving authority. There are two interesting aspects of the IRA organizational structure. The first is the dead wall of the set of rules. It is a dead wall because the rules are unchangeable and unalterable. The second is the interpretations of the rules. To avoid the risk of interpretations, the organization generally operates on the basis of precedence. Together, they create a bureaucracy where no information other than precedence is of any value. The rest of the organizational arrangements for the five activities discussed here are superfluous to the extent of legitimization of the decisions within the given set of rules. The process of legitimization, therefore, subjugates the actual purpose of a particular proposed action. A few specific features of the information management of such organizations deserve special attention.

1. The information management in such organizations is essentially inward-looking, be it in the approval of new research projects, monitoring and evaluation, or taking decisions about product and services. By inward-looking, we mean that actions are self-legitimizing within the organization. The loop of information flow, therefore, does not have any detour outside the organizational boundary. A researcher's project ideas are never scrutinized through a process of input from prospective users. Users of the IRA knowledge base are treated as 'others'. The result is a knowledge base in search of the user. This affects the quality of the research projects. The main reference points of the new project ideas are ongoing activities as reported in journals and presented in seminars and conferences. Novelty in the project ideas comes from interaction with prospective innovators. Working only on current and popular research problems helps to legitimize new projects. In fact, the basic ground of legitimization of any activity is whether it conforms to the current trend and popularity. However, there is no novelty in such a case. This is precisely the problem associated with monitoring and evaluation, and other activities discussed in the preceding paragraphs.

Growth in the new world order demands much more than mere conformity. To be able to remain ahead means to be able to do something that is not being done. The 'me too' mindset makes any organization a laggard in the global market. Thus, the information system should allow the flow of information to be processed for new ideas.

2. There is negligible value addition as information flows up or down the hierarchy. This means that the information is used only for decision-making. In all the critical activities discussed here information flows for approval or sanction alone. There are no loops wherein information is processed to add value. The same information, it has been observed, is used through informal channels with significant value addition. This value added information or processed knowledge, however, does not become a part of the knowledge base of the organization.

3. There is poor intra-organizational flow of information. As discussed, all the information loops end in their own department of origin after a detour for administrative decision-making. There is no interdepartmental flow of information. If we look at the total organizational map, we will see that there are forums for interdepartmental interactions. It is interesting to learn that most of them are virtually nonfunctional. In fact, the major schools under which the IRA's research activities are divided actually exist only on paper. There is no physical existence of such schools, nor are their functions defined.

4. Even as a decision-making arrangement, the flow of information is quite long-winded. Many of the nodes are repetitive and time-consuming. Also, most of the interceptions in the flow are actually a clerical requirement. Note that the information flow in any activity does not have any node for knowledge input. As a result, justification and legitimization of the project is only in terms of administrative and financial regulations. Such a system misses the urgency and importance of a research project. This is reflected in the time taken for sanctions. According to some IRA scientists, in many cases the final approval takes more than a year.

In the light of the above analysis, there is a definite indication that many changes are required to make IRA a modern knowledge organization. The mainstay of such changes is an organization that is outward-looking. It should be able to access information from the network of users and generators of knowledge. The next step is to process information for value addition instead of simple administrative decision-making. Finally, all this has to be done in real time so that the organization is able to capitalize on the value of information processed before it becomes outdated.

Benchmarking the best practices

Let us study a different perspective of IRA practices. According to available macro-level information, there is a huge demand for IRA output like new seed and plant varieties and also fertilizers. If the IRA has to maximize revenue it has to expand its seed and plant multiplication activities. This can be done by acquiring more farmland and more efficient use of the land in response to demand. The mainstay of this perspective is the revenue earned by the IRA and the client-satisfaction level (reflected in a huge demand for IRA output). This perspective leads to findings that are entirely different from our study. What is the source of this difference?

In our study, we did not begin the exercise armed with a specific set of performance indicators to evaluate IRA practices. Instead, we used the set of organizational principles to develop insights about the shortcomings of the existing practices. This helped us to identify issues like 'clarity about who are the clients'. In the process, we also discovered the redundancy in the administrative steps for project approval, and the banality of information flow up and down the administrative hierarchy. Once these problems were identified, the next step was identification of an alternative better (or best) practice.

Let us examine these observations in the light of the WAITRO study. Take the case of project approval in the IRA. In the discussion on the determination of service mix and ensuring quality of services, we drew attention to the importance of defining the target client and also the need for organized arrangements for interaction with clients.

We see that in the case of the IRA there is a need for further clarity on the clients of IRA services. A distinction is needed between beneficiaries and clients. Clarity is also needed regarding IRA output. Is it the new seed variety itself or the know-how for the new crop? Once the clients are defined, there have to be various forms of organized interactions between the IRA staff and the clients. The details of organizational arrangements have to be worked out by the IRA depending on their suitability to the specific organizational culture, ethos and history. The WAITRO study offers an understanding of best practices in this regard and can be used as a basic reference. We argued earlier about the virtues of practices like 'free on-site consultancy'. There could be many such effective practices. In fact, the actual practice that will be most suitable for the IRA will evolve over time if the IRA is vigilant about the effectiveness of practices for ensuring a meaningful interaction with its clients. Thus, we have benchmarked the essence of a practice instead of suggesting the actual logistics of the practice. The logistics of a practice are specific to an organization and have to be developed by the organization itself. What the benchmarking exercise has given us is the essence that is to be contained in the logistics.

One way of ensuring the effectiveness of practices would be to see if the new proposals contain substantial inputs from clients. For this purpose, the approval committee may seek specific information on the extensity and intensity of client interaction for a new proposal. This will have an implication on the project approval procedure. All those who have to approve a proposal will become less important. Instead, what is to be approved will become more important. Many steps in the process of approval will become redundant if there is more emphasis on the content of the proposal.

We have already pointed out that the long and complex process of project approval is more an administrative legitimization than an actual value addition to the content of the proposal. We have suggested how removing or merging various stages can reduce the number of steps to two. Arrangements for close interaction (which is completely absent at present) with clients will ensure the content of the proposal and administrative legitimization will eventually become redundant.

Governance of IRT[16]

The Institutes of Research in Textiles (IRTs) were created under the joint initiative of the government and the industry. They are a chain of eight research institutes specializing in the different technological aspects of the textile industry. The respective industry associations manage the IRTs. The government provides funds as a grant (about 50 per cent) as well as for research projects in areas considered important by both the industry and the government.

Industries as well as the government think that IRTs do not propose many meaningful research projects, and even projects completed do not reach the shop floor of the industry. The project team was asked to investigate the matter and suggest organizational remedies. The team was briefed about the weak interactions among IRTs, and among IRTs, the government and the industries.

As in the case of the IRA, we did not begin the study with a set of quantitative performance indicators for a set of given processes and practices. Instead, we planned to locate the most critical process that would affect the research activities of the IRTs and the delivery of research results to the clients. We started tracing the route of research projects from the formulation to the completion stage via the approval procedure. While tracing the route, we were again governed by the basic organizational principles outlined in Chapter 6. In this particular case,

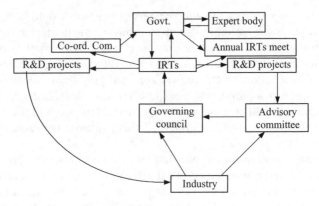

Figure 7.10   Existing structure of interaction

we began by examining the communication network among the government departments, the industry associations, and the IRTs.

The general communication network of the IRTs with the government and the industry is shown in Figure 7.10. There could be a little variation for different IRTs, but the basic framework remains the same.

The communication and coordination network has three junctions, namely the IRTs, the industry, and the government. Since IRTs are not one single entity, inter-IRT interaction has to have separate institutional and organizational arrangements. Inter-IRT interaction, therefore, adds another dimension to the network. We shall take up all three dimensions separately.

Inter-IRT interaction

Modern-day industrial R&D is no longer a lone inventor's excellence but teamwork. Even 'teamwork' or 'group work' is not adequate to explain modern R&D. The meanings of these words have become more varied today. Teams are no longer restricted to a single R&D institution. Instead, industrial R&D is done by an inter-institutional network. The advantage of such an inter-institutional network-based team is a pool of physical and human resources that is created with the ultimate purpose of knowledge-generation for mutual benefit. It also makes good sense *vis-à-vis* financial resource management.

Independent instead of interdependent functioning of IRTs

There are three main junctures where some kind of inter-IRT interactions take place:

1. Cross-representation of IRT directors in their governing councils
2. Annual IRT meet
3. Coordination committee at the government level

These three junctures play important roles in building up interactions among IRTs in their own way, albeit, to a limited extent. The representation of the director of one IRT in another IRT's governing council will remain a superficial networking until and unless it results in networking down the line to the activities of the IRTs. At present, there is no institutional mechanism for encouraging such networking.

What is exchanged at these forums is information about who is doing what. This information is used for taking decisions on the future activities of the respective IRTs. Thus, if an IRT has got a good response from industries to a particular service, for other IRTs this is information that helps them in taking up a similar programme. The funding from the government for such a programme also becomes easy, because it is already legitimized by the initial success of the initiator IRT.

Our interaction with industries brought out an important dimension of industrial research. Talking about new machine development as an example of R&D projects, the general view of the industries was that their existing capability was enough to develop the machine. R&D was required in the critical components of such machines. According to the industries, the IRTs were independently taking up small aspects of one such component, whereas, it required not only a series or chain of R&D on a component as a whole but also on all the critical components at the same time. More specifically, many such components need R&D in metallurgy for developing new alloys. The IRTs do not have much capability in metallurgical R&D. If their capability in machine design, based on the specific needs of the industries, could be used together with R&D from a metallurgical research institute, a more significant breakthrough might be possible. This means bringing together many IRTs to create a knowledge pool and also accessing the capability of research institutions for further extending the combined knowledge pool of the IRTs. The total knowledge pool thus created is to be integrated under a project for achieving one major goal.

This goal cannot be achieved as of now because the present level and nature of inter-IRT interaction does not leave any such scope. An interdependent structure would require functional interaction deep down the line of organizational hierarchy. Presently, it is just restricted to the level of IRT Directors. The present level of interaction leads to information exchange and subsequent decision-making of an individual IRT as an independent entity. It does not allow the use of information for the generation of knowledge where the IRTs do not take decisions independently but operate in an interdependent structure.

Instruments for enforcing inter-IRT interaction

The most important instrument that can help achieve a cooperative mode of research is undertaking projects that use the core competence of the S&T personnel across the IRTs. This would mean conceiving projects involving a higher level of technological knowledge than the present practice where the knowledge content of the projects is limited to the capability available within an IRT. Under the present circumstances, the IRTs function within an organizational structure that is not conducive or amenable to such multi-institutional projects.

Institutionalization of interdependence

There are three major components of the institutionalization of inter-IRT coordination:

1. It is necessary to build up an organizational structure with empowerment down the line in both research activity and the administrative aspects of decision-making. This has to accompany suitable incentives and encouragement for committing inter-institutional major projects. There is an alarmingly low level of interaction among the scientific and technical personnel of most IRTs. Such interaction is even lower across the hierarchy. Such internal interactions are essential for meaningful networking with the outer world. A suitable organizational arrangement with empowerment and internal interaction has to be designed and institutionally enforced in the IRTs.
2. Much of this problem can be tackled by projectization of the IRT activities and delegating authority and responsibility to the project leader for selecting the project team and executing the project.
3. Another important way of promoting inter-IRT coordination is through the funding pattern of the projects. Setting up a technology mission and giving priority funding to inter-institutional projects will help inter-IRT interaction. This, however, has to be undertaken at the governmental level.

These issues will come up again when we discuss IRT–government and IRT–industry interactions. They will be tackled along with the suggested organizational structure.

Government–IRT interaction

Funding of IRT activities is the main instrument of government–IRT interaction. The government is represented in the governing councils of the IRTs. The inter-IRT coordination committee is also located in the concerned government department. It gives the concerned ministry a platform to translate the technology-related issues and policies into action. It also helps the ministry to assess the capabilities of the industries in terms of their technological priorities. This organizational arrangement helps the ministry in the process of resource mobilization.

How these advantages are capitalized upon, however, depends on the perceived role of the government in industrial technology research and associated management practices. The existing pattern of IRT–government interaction is styled to suit the traditional role of government as resource allocator. In the era of liberalization, the government's role is more that of a resource creator as opposed to a resource allocator. The new role demands that the government should act not as a benevolent funder but as an initiator and actor for striking up a partnership among the industry, the IRT and the government. This triangular relationship does not begin with the idea of accessing the fund available with the government. The beginning is the initiation of a strategic plan for the creation of a competitive knowledge base by defining the specific roles to be played by all three partners. Funding forms a component of this strategic planning. At this point, the government can use the fiscal instrument for mobilizing funds, and bring in institutional finance to create a corpus fund for the defined purpose. The government funding this way may become even larger than the present commitment.

The present arrangement for the allocation of funds is quite simple. An expert committee constituted by the government for this purpose justifies the proposals sent by the IRTs. IRTs are the interface between the government and the industries. The logic by which the present arrangement is supposed to function is that industries articulate their technological needs to the IRTs, and the IRTs in turn access the funds from the government for the research and/or capital equipment components of such demands. Once that is done there should not be any problem in releasing funds to the respective IRTs, barring normal delays in the movement of files. This is the major form of formal interaction between the government and the IRTs. Any other form, like representation of the government or government-nominated persons in the governing council of the IRTs, is mainly decorative and there is no functional relationship between the two.

The coordination committee is another forum where the IRTs' activities are reviewed. The meetings of this committee are irregular, and without any representation from the industry the views and decisions of the committee members are likely to be partial. It is interesting to note that there is no direct interaction between the government and IRTs where it is most required.

The concerned ministry is not expected to have in-house expertise for the selection of R&D projects from the proposals submitted by IRTs. Expert views are sought annually for helping the selection process. In matters related to R&D, project selection is a serious process. This is evident from the knowledge-generation part of the model described earlier. The IRTs' interaction with the expert body is indirect and via the ministry. Instead, this should be direct and it should be institutionalized in such a way that an expert body becomes an integral part of IRTs instead of being an annual formality.

Partnership among government, industry and IRTs

We have already argued for a new role of the government in the post-liberalization economy. The crux of the new role, in the context of IRTs and the technological competitiveness of the textile industry is to build up a strategy with a triangular partnership. One important way is to develop a technology mission in association with the industry, associated trade bodies (like export association, chambers of commerce, etc.) and financial institutions. While this has to be done at the ministerial level, an appropriate task force has to be created for selection, and monitoring the progress of the selected projects under the mission. The task force will have to be the interface between the ministry and the IRTs and will be constituted of experts and representatives from the appropriate industry segment, the IRTs and the ministry. This will be a new version of the present expert committee and the coordination committee, and will essentially translate the government's policy and the technology mission into a technological action programme. A scrutiny of the project proposals, approval and recommendation for funding would be the main terms of reference of this committee.

The purpose behind such a forum, as an interface between the IRTs and the government, is threefold. The first purpose is to bring the industry closer to the ministry so that direct input from the industry in matters related to IRTs and technological priorities is available to the ministry. The second aim is that IRTs should have direct interaction with the experts for the project scrutiny and selection process. The third purpose is that the IRTs' interaction with the ministry will then be through this forum. The last purpose would make IRTs more autonomous *vis-à-vis* the ministry. This is essential to direct more attention to the problem of R&D management, which is different from the management of a ministry.

Industry–IRT coordination

The issue of industry–IRT coordination needs an understanding of the structure of the industry. The following are some of the salient points that will help us to arrive at our suggestions for a structured coordination.

Structure of the industry

1. The industry is widely segmented – from growing cotton to the finished fabric.
2. The composite structure of the industry (integrating mainly ginning to the finished fabric) has broken up.
3. The decline of composite mills was quickened by the rise of power looms in the decentralized sector. The ginning and processing segment of the industry also became decentralized.
4. The opening up of the economy has made the industry technologically vulnerable to international competition.
5. Many surviving composite mills have gone for state-of-the-art modernization. The power loom sector has been surviving on low-cost production. They are also being threatened by low-cost substitutes from overseas competitors.

Implication and expectation from IRTs

1. With the impending doom in the composite sector, the mills' interaction with IRTs has declined considerably. Those who have modernized find the IRTs' capability of little use for their state-of-the-art technology. Their main demand from IRTs is for a few ordinary testing and certification services.
2. The decentralized sector essentially operates at the lower end of the technology – needing only ordinary services.
3. The decentralized sector does not have a strong enough representation in the IRTs to influence R&D activities.

Structural constraints of IRTs

IRTs face two major problems. In the composite mill structure, different segments of the industrial activities used to be under one enterprise or under one roof. So IRTs could address technological problems for different segments at the same time. In a decentralized structure, IRTs have to attend different enterprises for different technology segments. This has diffused the IRTs' effort in interaction and coordination with industries. Secondly, in a reorganized industry, the main expectations from the IRTs being ordinary testing services and extension work, IRTs have become more service-oriented than R&D-oriented.

Add financial pressure to this scenario IRTs survive basically on maximizing revenue from testing and extension services. As a result getting into R&D in advanced technology areas become either nil or negligible and sporadic. The situation has been further aggravated by a continuous depletion of human resources. The R&D activities having taken a back seat and unattractive financial remuneration in IRT jobs, IRTs find themselves in an unenviable situation as far as human resources are concerned.

Industry representatives did not hesitate to concede that they are casual as far as R&D activities of the IRTs are concerned. A large cross-section of the industry representatives have also opined that today's situation demands more concentration on R&D by IRTs by conceiving a major technological programme in collaboration and help from the government.

The nature of the major project has to be much different from the present piecemeal R&D activities of the IRTs. As expressed by the industry representatives, the need is for R&D on a full set technology rather than a small component of a technological problem. To take up a major project in a full set technology, a pool of expertise needs to be mobilized not only from the IRTs but also from other research organizations all over the country.

Implications on organizational arrangements

Decentralized sectors being the major components of the textile industry, the IRTs' R&D activities have to focus on the technological issues of this sector. At the same time, IRTs should not be expected to organize finance or execute extension programmes for this sector. This part of the activities should be left to the different agencies of the state government. These agencies should access the IRTs' help as and when required. The IRTs can create a separate unit to take care of this function. To reflect upon this sector's needs in the IRTs' R&D activities, there can be suitable representation of the state government in the governing council of the IRTs.

As discussed earlier, in matters related to the IRTs, the industry does not have any direct interaction with the government. This is essential to revitalize the interest of the industry in the IRTs' activities.

New organizational arrangements

In the beginning, we described the existing organizational arrangements necessary for a triangular interaction among the government, the industry and the IRTs. On the basis of the observed needs in a changed scenario, we are presenting an alternative organizational arrangement for a more effective triangular relationship among the three (Figure 7.11).

The mission is to be executed by a task force, which will be constituted of representatives from industries, trade bodies, experts, financial institutions and IRTs. The permanent secretariat of the task force may be constituted of the IRTs.

The expert committee that scrutinizes the project proposal from the IRTs and the coordination committee are to be replaced by a committee of experts and representatives from the government, financial

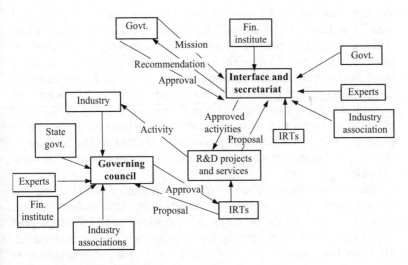

Figure 7.11 Proposed structure of interaction

institutions, IRTs and industries. This committee will be permanent in nature and will review, recommend and monitor the progress of the projects under the technology mission. The inclusion of financial institutions is a major feature of this structure. Till now there has been no involvement of financial institutions in the activities of IRTs.

Commercialization of the R&D results will require funding. In case of a new textile machinery, funding will be much more critical for the commercialization of any R&D results. The involvement of financial institutions will smoothen the process. Accessing venture capital will also become easier.

Another important feature of the suggested structure is that it will relieve the government from day-to-day monitoring of the IRTs. The government instead gets a major role in policy formulation, mobilization of funds and building up a technology mission.

At the IRT level, we have suggested strengthening the governing council for primary inputs for project guidance and selection by the inclusion of financial institutions and state government agencies. At present, the state government is not involved in the activities of IRTs. This is particularly important when IRTs are seen as a major source of technological inputs for the decentralized sector, the development of which comes under the jurisdiction of the state government.

Benchmarking the best practices

We have looked into the governance of the IRTs. Governance has been seen as a flow of information and decision-making through value addition to the information. Close interactions among the stakeholders have been used as the necessary organizational principle for examining the existing structure and suggesting a new structure. In this case, the stakeholders are the government, the industry and the IRTs. It was not difficult to detect that the major problem facing the governance of IRTs had been constrained interactions among the IRTs, derived interactions between the government departments and the industry associations, and casual interactions between the industry associations and the IRTs.

This is a case where the funder (the government) is not the client. At the same time, the government decides about the R&D projects that are to be undertaken by the IRTs. The IRTs are supposed to submit proposals for new projects after getting inputs from the industry associations. There are two important junctions in the new governance structure, as suggested by the study team, where all stakeholders meet. The first is at the government level, and the second is at the IRT level. The basic idea behind the structure has been to bring both the funders and the users of the IRT services together in different forums.

It is also to be noted that the mainstay of the benchmarking exercise has been clearly defining the clients of the IRT services. Once that is done, the essence of the best practice is to create a logistic arrangement to facilitate closer interactions among the stakeholders and the clients.

8
Effective Organization is Learning Organization

Recapitulation

RTO–client interaction is an organizational process where knowledge-generation and delivery of the research results is a part of the dynamic partnership between the two. An organization's growth depends upon its ability to generate knowledge from information – more so, in the case of an RTO, whose main function is to generate and market knowledge.

We have focused on the organizational principles of innovative and dynamic organizations, where the organization develops the ability to access, process and utilize information to generate knowledge. This requires investment in R&D for building a knowledge base and also a closer interaction with the industry for transferring the generated knowledge in the form of products and processes. This needs to be understood in a comprehensive way. Activities that are considered effective in today's context may not remain so in a future point in time. The ability to meet the current needs of the client industries, therefore, is only a partial account of the effectiveness of any research organization. RTOs have to have the ability to address the future and the emerging technological needs of the client industries. They have to be in the process of continuously upgrading their knowledge base so that they can address the new and emerging technological requirements of the industry. This needs strategy, planning and effort because the generation of knowledge is not instantaneously responsive to the industry's technological needs. Hence, effectiveness in RTO–client interaction means that the research organizations have to remain ahead in their knowledge level compared to the clients whom they would be serving.

RTOs should also be prepared to cater to the industry's future technological requirements. They have to invest in R&D to build this capability.

As stated by Cohen and Levinthal, R&D has two faces – it does not only generate innovations, but also develops learning and absorptive capabilities (Cohen and Levinthal 1989, 1990).

Another important aspect of industrial technology research is that there is no way of assigning market price to the new knowledge that the RTO is expected to generate. It is the clients who, as the users of the research results, determine the price. In the case of technological knowledge, market prices will be there only for common research results. However, a growth-oriented firm is not looking for common market knowledge. Firms normally expect common market-knowledge-based services from RTOs in the form of certain routine activities, which they are not interested in undertaking within their premises. A dynamic firm would expect certain new knowledge-based services from RTOs, services that it does not possess and is not willing to generate on its own. In both cases, the RTOs are expected to possess the knowledge base that is either equal to or more than their clients.

The nature of services provided by RTOs ranges from totally physical-resource-based, like routine testing and standardization to a human-resource-based service like new knowledge in the form of new products and processes. What we understand by a physical-resource-based service is that there is hardly any scope for human initiatives in the services provided by the RTO. There is no value addition to the services in the form of knowledge inputs. Physical-resource-based services are basically machine-oriented services, that is, services in which manpower is utilized for operating machines. Maybe an RTO can survive with physical-resource-based services, but in the long run, for its growth, the RTO will have to progressively switch over to human-resource-based services. An RTO has to make use of human knowledge inputs and in coordination with physical resources it should be able to contribute value addition to the services it provides. A research organization's growth depends upon the value addition it is able to offer to the services it provides to its clients. This becomes more pertinent now with the changing scenario with respect to the role and relevance of these RTOs. Firms are into new competition, which involves market-shaping activities rather than market-reacting activities (Best 1990). Productive organizations are described by Best as those that strategize their activities at various levels, to have superior production knowledge manifested in superior products and processes that give the organization a competitive edge (Best 1990). This depends upon the ability of the organization to develop unique knowledge assets that are not available with the competitors.

Knowledge and organization[17]

Knowledge is considered the only meaningful economic resource of the post-capitalist or knowledge society (Drucker 1993). Firms are continuously in the process of enhancing their knowledge base for creating unique knowledge-based assets. Thus, the relationship between RTOs and firms has to be seen in this new milieu where the RTOs have to continuously upgrade their knowledge base to meet the new knowledge requirements of the firms. The core function of any RTO is to provide service to its clients and this is dependent upon the knowledge base of the RTO, which in turn is dependent upon the human capital that an organization has as its asset. To remain effective, therefore, simply means that RTOs have to remain several steps ahead of the industry clients in terms of the level of knowledge. They also have to have preparedness to be able to address the future needs of the industries. This, of course, is in conjunction with the present technological services to the industries.

Organizational arrangement and practices, therefore, are crucial issues for the effectiveness of an RTO's activities. The organization has to be vigilant and alert. It should be able to perceive changes and build an internal dynamism to adapt to changes in organizational practices. It should accommodate clients and fast-changing technological requirements. Closer interaction between RTOs and industry clients would help the clients to develop confidence in the RTOs' capabilities to access such knowledge-based technological services from the RTOs. Through closer interaction and active participation, the market mechanism is superseded by the organizational mechanism for understanding the present and future demand pattern of the industries and gearing up the knowledge-generating system accordingly.

Organizations have people with information, knowledge and skill. This knowledge is scattered in an organization. A dynamic organization as a first step has to convert its manpower into a human resource. What we are trying to say is that manpower is a collection of individuals with different educational backgrounds and orientations, whereas human resource is something that the organization makes out of this by bringing them together and orienting their individual knowledge to the organizational goal. To sustain and enhance the knowledge base of the human resource, the organization has to utilize them for achieving the strategic goals of the organization.

Is the organization also learning with the enhanced knowledge base of its individual workers? To put the question in a different way, is the knowledge embodied in the manpower as well as in the organization?

The question is important because the learning or knowledge in the possession of an organization is not the sum of all the individuals' learning (Fiol and Lyles 1985). This individual knowledge or capability cannot be construed as organizational capability or resource. It becomes an organizational resource only when this individual knowledge base gets related to a common organizational knowledge base. To turn this individual knowledge into an organizational asset is an organizational process. As mentioned earlier, organizations have to convert their manpower into a human resource. This is an organizational process, where an individual's goals have to be oriented towards the goals of the organization and the individual knowledge base has to become a part of the organizational knowledge base. Only then does the knowledge base contribute to the organization's growth.

This process of transformation has to be a part of the organizational strategy. This requires effort in the form of planning and financial commitment. It has to be part of the overall planning of resource mobilization and allocation. The strategy for human resource development has to be worked out in accordance with the organizational goals and objectives to be achieved. Human resource generation, development and sustenance should be seen in this context. Human resource generation has to be planned and coordinated with various other organizational activities. The recruitment process is the channel through which an RTO can get the set of people it wants. In most of the RTOs that we studied, the rules for hiring and discharging people were very rigid. This process surely restricts the choice of getting the right set of people. Flexibility helps in selecting the right people, when human resource development is part of the RTO's strategic planning.

Building a learning RTO

Through recruitment, the organization gets a set of people who differ in their educational qualifications and experience. Each individual has his own understanding of organizational requirements and knowledge base. 'Knowledge and expertise is dispersed throughout the organization and is often closely held by individuals or work units' (Choo 1996). From here, the organization has to take them through various organizational processes to transform them into an organizational resource. To evolve a common understanding, it is essential to have an organizational structure that ensures a free exchange and flow of information among people at different levels through formal and informal channels.

This facilitates the process of developing a common understanding and beliefs among them. A decentralized structure with accountability is found to encourage more participation and commitment in people towards their work. This helps to involve people in the process of organizational growth and development.

The organization can motivate people through certain incentives in the form of promotions with additional responsibilities. Additional responsibility and direct participation help in making an individual more committed towards his work. Evaluation followed by recognition for good work encourages people to get more involved in organizational activities. It is also very important to have a correlation between performance evaluation of the personnel and the broad goals and objectives of the organization. If an RTO's objective is to cater to the technological requirements of its clients, then scientific publications should not be a criterion for promotion. The evaluation process also either orients or disorients people from relating their personal goals and knowledge base to the organizational goals and knowledge system. Attractive career prospects in the form of research in new and emerging areas can help in getting the right set of people, and also help in retaining them. Formal organizational training programmes can again orient people with a certain common understanding.

This is where the manpower begins to visualize itself as a part of the organization. For an organization to understand and react to the external changes, an organization's members should have a common understanding of what the organization is and what it is doing (Choo 1996). This will help the people to relate their knowledge and understanding to the organization's requirements. A change in the organization is not possible unless all the major decision-makers learn together, share their beliefs and goals, and are committed to taking the actions necessary for change (Stata 1989). Organizations learn through individuals but it is through organizational strategy and policy mechanisms that organizations have to retain this learning (Stata 1989). This is a process of institutionalization by which an organization does not have to totally depend upon individual knowledge base.

People have to be involved at various levels in organizational decisions, whether it is in selecting projects, or internal capability-building, or performance evaluation systems, or in interaction with clients. 'All organizational actions are initiated by decisions, and all decisions are commitments to action' (Choo 1996). Thus, people are jointly committed to implement the decisions taken.

An individual becomes a part of the organization's human resources only when he is able to orient his knowledge base to the organizational goals and objectives and becomes a constituent of a knowledge system. It is in this context that the importance of the organization needs to be understood. An organization can create human resources out of individuals by establishing a synergy between individual skill and knowledge base. This requires an effort on the part of the organization to transform individually scattered manpower into a human resource.

Organizational practices can either facilitate or deter the process of converting individual knowledge into collective knowledge. For this transformation, it is very essential that people get the opportunity to share their ideas and experiences, so that there is scope for value addition to the information that is exchanged. Teamwork and collective participation in organizational activities gives individuals an opportunity to come out of their shell and share their ideas. The organizational transformation process is 'conversion of human capital into structural capital. [It] is an epistemological transformation in the tacit–explicit dimension and an ontological transformation in the individual–collective dimension' (Perez-Bustamante 1999). When individuals give expression and shape to their ideas they are bound by certain limitations. Human cognition is limited by 'bounded rationality'. An organization can provide the necessary domain for overcoming such limitations (Simon 1976). What an organization can do is to provide the domain for enhancement, expression, and sustainability of this human-embodied knowledge base so that it becomes a resource. An individual's ability gets converted into an organizational resource through the organizational process of transformation (Nonaka and Takeuchi 1995). Individuals then become human resources that can be related to the organizational goals. Much more than the physical assets, it is this intangible human-embodied resource that differentiates one organization from another in terms of competitive advantage. The human resource development programme of an organization, therefore, plays a crucial role in the effectiveness and growth of an organization. This helps an organization to build its knowledge base that gives it a competitive advantage.

Human resource as the key

The utilization of human resources has to be seen in the context of the research organizations' role in knowledge-generation and delivery to its clients. Once the manpower is transformed into a human resource with the commitment to achieve organizational goals, the organization has to sustain this by facilitating the process of interaction, both internal and external to the organization. In many RTOs, internal seminars and both formal and informal discussions among people are encouraged and the outcomes are recorded for further action. External links with university, industry and other research institutions open the channel for the flow of information. In one of the RTOs, it was found that the RTO's personnel were the teaching faculty of the concerned department of the university. The students got placement in the industry once they passed out of the university. They acted as a link between the industry and the RTO. This external link ensured a continuous exchange of information and also brought the clients and the RTO personnel closer.

In the Japanese prefecture laboratories, clients have direct interaction with the technical people and discuss their problems. It is known as 'on-site consultancy', that is, one-to-one interaction with the clients. This has been found to be very effective in articulating the clients' problems and finally delivering the results to the clients.

It is important to have access to information in the research field and also from the industry so that the RTO personnel understand the problem better. The organization has to encourage people to take the initiative. The ability to access, process and utilize information for knowledge-generation is human-embodied. The more an organization is able to make use of the knowledge base of their human resource the more it gets an opportunity to enhance the knowledge base of its personnel. The organization can facilitate this process by encouraging internal and external interaction among people. This ensures a flow of information from various channels. People have to choose the information for processing and decide on how to use it and for what. This whole process involves active participation and initiatives from the people. A dynamic RTO, which has to face competition, will make use of the existing knowledge base of its human resource to generate new knowledge. This might mean a new application of the existing knowledge, or new products and processes for the clients. Closer interaction with clients helps RTO personnel to understand and articulate the requirements of their clients.

An RTO needs to identify and prioritize the areas of its research activities and the delivery of research results to the clients. How are research areas identified and how are they prioritized? The client's active participation is very important for an RTO to evolve a strategy in terms of whether to venture into new and emerging areas or to strengthen the existing research areas. The organizational practices for either venture in terms of financial investment for human and physical resource requirements would be different. The involvement of clients as members of an organization's decision-making board has been found to be an important factor as far as delivery of results to the clients are concerned. Clients' involvement ensures an external commitment because the RTOs do not have to look for the clients once their research results are ready. As stated earlier, RTOs have to strategize their research activities based on the clients' present as well as future requirements. In any dynamic organization, all these are concurrent activities. There has to be strategic planning with the necessary human and physical resources in order to reach strategic decisions in research areas.

Thus, it is human resource that holds the key in an organization because physical resource, although no less important, is inert. Also, physical resource needs to be operated upon for capitalizing on its capability. It is human resource that has the skill and knowledge of making use of the physical resource. In addition, human resource has flexible use in contrast to physical resource, which has a rigidly defined capability or functions. The knowledge or skill of the human resource is not specific to a particular use, and the same knowledge base and skill can be used for more than one purpose – in fact, for unlimited purposes. The knowledge and skill of the human resource can be enhanced, developed and directed. It is the learning capability of the human resource that distinguishes it from the other resources and makes it the most important factor in today's post-capitalist society.

The knowledge base of an organization is enriched by interactions and opens up opportunities for the creation of new knowledge. The organization has to be structured so that it promotes such interactions and becomes conducive to the creation of new knowledge, because in the long run, the organization can survive and grow only if it is a knowledge-creating organization. Organizations are continuously learning through their human resource but what differentiates one organization from another is the difference in their strategy, effort, intention and learning ability. It is important to translate this individual learning into organizational achievements.

Organizational learning is a process through which knowledge is internalized. The ability to learn and internalize their learning is something that differentiates one organization from another. Theoretically also, the role of the human resource in economic growth and technological advancement is important. A 'learning organization' has to develop certain organization-specific capabilities. In the present context, an organization's competitive strength is determined by its ability to create, acquire, process and assimilate knowledge in a manner different from that of its competitors. To gain a competitive edge, an organization has to develop organization-specific assets through its strategic human resource management. Learning can take place in several ways, like training, internal and external linkages for acquiring and processing information and upgrading technical qualifications. The internalization process requires an organizational arrangement to nurture the retention and application of the knowledge so generated. Knowledge accumulation or even its sharing requires a longer period of association (Aoki 1986). Another important dimension to organizational learning is the ability to access, process and assimilate information for decision-making purposes (Choo 1996). Why is an organization necessary for this? An organization can facilitate interaction within as well as with the outside world. It is a process that takes place over a period of time, and it requires planned coordination within the organization.

Learning is a conscious effort through which knowledge is accumulated. It is the skill that gives shape to this knowledge in the form of a product, process, or design. Learning can be understood in terms of self-learning (learning by doing) and through interaction (formal education and organizational training). Economists have examined learning and the associated skill development in an attempt to explain the development of new industries and technologies (Rosenberg 1976, 1982). They attribute this growth to the creation of certain formalized R&D structures as seats of learning. Productivity enhancement through repetitive jobs (Arrow 1962b) and incremental innovation through accumulation of knowledge (Dosi 1988; Nelson and Winter 1982) are also perceived as forms of learning. Management literature tries to explain innovation and competitive advantage as a feature of a learning organization (Dogdson 1993).

We are dealing with learning as an organizational process. The role of the organization is in managing and coordinating the process and the outcome of learning. An organization can be said to contain a reservoir of knowledge created around individuals. An innovative organization needs to manage this resource very effectively for generating innovations. A technology that is generated by an RTO is not merely a bundle of physical artifacts. It requires tacit and codified knowledge built around individuals. This knowledge can make better use of machines.

Individual knowledge to organizational knowledge

The conversion of individual knowledge to an organizational domain is a transformation process that can be termed as organizational learning.

It is a process in which individuals share their insights, knowledge and ideas to develop a common understanding (Stata 1989). Organizations enrich their knowledge base through learning. A good knowledge base helps an organization in knowledge-generation. In the long run, the organization is able to face external challenges in a more efficient way. The internal capability to exploit, evaluate and utilize external knowledge is an organization's absorptive capacity, which is a priori knowledge in the related field (Cohen and Levinthal 1990). Even to know what information one has to use or to understand its relevance for the organization, it is essential to develop internal capability. So, it is important for a research organization to have a knowledge base in order to be able to translate the client's requirement into research activity.

RTOs adopt various practices to build internal capabilities. Some RTOs prefer to appoint experts in the field whereas others train people to generate expertise. By taking up projects in new and emerging areas, RTOs give opportunity to their staff to take initiatives and experiment with new ideas. We observed this mostly in cases where the industry was well developed and the demand put forward by the industry was quite challenging. Another important practice has been learning through collaboration, in which projects are undertaken jointly with the industry. In addition to this, many RTOs encourage their personnel to go for higher studies. Several RTOs involve their clients in the decision-making process and encourage closer interaction between the RTO personnel and the clients through both formal and informal channels. Thus, RTOs do not work in isolation.

An innovative or productive organization will strive to be a learning organization – 'skilled at creating, acquiring and transferring knowledge and modifying its behavior to reflect new knowledge and insights' (Gravin 1993). As discussed earlier, research is expected to generate knowledge and a knowledge-generating organization is one that is able to develop, sustain and utilize its human resource.

An important structural characteristic of any learning organization is information flow within the organization and access to information from the external world. This is essentially a part of the information-processing activity for which both inter- and intra-organizational flow of information is kept alive. An organization can in fact be defined in terms of channels of information flow. The network of such channels is the organizational structure.

Information can be generated internally or it can be accessed from sources outside the organization. A dynamic organization will have information from both internal and external sources. In other words, the design of the organizational structure will be such that it can access and process information from within as well as from outside the organization. In a learning organization, the accessed information undergoes a metamorphosis with value addition through interpretation. It is in this process that the organization takes advantage of human resources by overcoming the problem of 'bounded rationality' and accumulating knowledge input from a resource pool. Organizational efficiency is critically dependent on the extent of value addition in the process of information flow across the organizational hierarchy. Traditionally, such information flow will essentially mean approval or sanction, that is, a file will move up from the bottom for the approval of somebody up in the hierarchy. The information will then come back to its origin with an instruction. This is an example of a bureaucratic organization where human resources and its function is desired to be as rigid as it is in the case of physical resources. The human resources, in such an organization, do not act as a resource and as a knowledge-generating agency. Such organizations will be stable but moribund over time. On the contrary, in organizations where information flow is with value addition, the process of knowledge-generation is put into action. Simultaneously, an organizational dynamics is created by which human resources become more enriched, and the organization's quest for more and more information increases. The organization's purpose becomes more to access information and seek opportunities for gainful application of generated knowledge. In fact, the application of knowledge becomes a part of the process of knowledge-generation. Another aspect of the new dynamics is that the organizational structure changes along the line of increasing quest for more extensive and intensive knowledge. The organizational structure, therefore, can remain neither stable nor rigid over time. One indicator of a dynamic knowledge-creating organization, therefore, is whether the organization has undergone structural changes over time.

We have argued that a dynamic organization will use its human resources for the generation of information and its processing for the generation of new knowledge. The basic function is generation of new knowledge and at the same time creation of opportunities of applications of new knowledge (Mrinalini and Nath 2000). Dynamic organizations cannot afford to be bureaucratic, nor can their structure remain unchanged over a period of time. The critical distinction of such organizations is that the organization has to offer something which others are not offering. Compare it with a firm which may compete with several other firms selling the same products. An organization in the business of knowledge-generation cannot sell the same knowledge that another organization is selling. We are talking about R&D organizations. R&D organizations can be characterized as organizations mandated to the generation and application of knowledge. It is essentially human-resource-based and the knowledge generated is generally human-embodied.

Implications for RTOs

An RTO will have to involve itself in three activities that are interlinked. The organization has to keep abreast with the present and future trends in the world, for the knowledge-generation process. This is followed by knowledge application, where finally knowledge is transformed for use in the production sphere. The organization has to be fully aware of the new possibilities and potentialities of application of new knowledge and also new application of existing knowledge. The transformation of knowledge into the field of production is as complex and fuzzy as the generation of knowledge. Success here depends as much on the right partner as on the substance of the knowledge.

For a smooth delivery of research results to the client it is important that the client is involved right from the beginning. Closer interaction between the RTO personnel and the client facilitates a sharing of information and a better articulation of the problem. This again involves a set of people who have the unique capability of reconverting the research results into the client's products. The personnel should not only be capable of understanding the research results but they should also be able to translate it into the client's requirements. On the basis of the information accessed from these two activities, the organization has to draw a strategy for pursuing a particular trajectory and field of knowledge, keeping the potentiality and capability of its use in the sphere of production. Thus, the organization's research strategy has to be linked with the present and future requirements of the clients. Therefore, the extent of information accessing, processing and use play a critical role in an R&D organization. Information management has to be more efficient and intensive in an R&D organization.

We are looking for a dynamic RTO that can perceive and act upon the fast-changing external scenario. The basic function of an RTO is to generate knowledge and deliver the knowledge application to the production system. To establish its relevance to its clients, it has to continuously upgrade its knowledge base. The knowledge base is human-embodied and a dynamic organization, through its organizational practices, will convert its manpower into human resource. It will use its human resources for knowledge-generation. The RTO has to not only build its internal capability but also has to have the ability to convince its clients about its capability to serve them. For this, the RTO has to understand its client's requirements and then translate them into an R&D activity, and finally give its client the end product. In addition to this, the RTO has to develop and sustain capability to create new knowledge to keep its clients abreast of future requirements. How an organization performs depends upon its capability to build and enhance this knowledge base. So, any organization's growth in terms of knowledge competitiveness is determined by the investment the organization makes in generating and utilizing its human resource.

9
An RTO as a Vigilant Organization: A Postscript

We have argued that benchmarking the organizational practices is helpful in enhancing the organizational effectiveness of RTOs. The process of enhancing organizational effectiveness, however, does not end there. Implementation of the best organizational practices replacing the existing inefficient practices is not an easy task. As it is evident from the benchmarking (BM) exercises in Chapter 7, implementation of best practices means restructuring the responsibility, accountability, reporting, tasks, opportunities, reward and redeployment of manpower. Briefly, it means transformation of power structure within an organization. Many of these exercises may go against the convention that is part of the history of the organization. An organization, which opts for benchmarking exercise for its organizational practices, has to be ready for many surprises that are likely to be discovered when practices are compared. It also has to be ready for breaking the inertia that an organization accumulates against changes of accustomed practices. For successful BM exercises an organization has to be non-complacent, change oriented, and open to learning from others. These are the symptoms of a vigilant organization, which we propose to define as an organization seeking excellence. A vigilant organization continuously seeks critical reviews of its practices and adopts the best that may ensure excellence. Such organizations are more open to criticism than praises of its practices. Conceptually, a vigilant organization envelops the concept of a learning organization. But a learning organization will not be enough for a successful BM exercise. In this chapter we try to draw a distinction between the two concepts to develop a working definition of a vigilant organization. We begin with the contemporary understanding of a learning organization.

Learning organization

The concept of learning organization has evolved around the urgency of attaining competitive advantage of business enterprises. Recent developments, however, extend the concept beyond business enterprises to include efficiency of varieties of organizations. In the present study, we have not looked at an RTO as a business enterprise that is engaged in seeking profit but as an organization engaged in the business of generation and dissemination of knowledge, and in the process generating revenue to sustain and grow. In doing so, an RTO has to legitimize its existence by remaining ahead of the knowledge pool available with its clients and other RTOs. We have argued earlier that the physical-asset-based knowledge in possession of any RTO may help it generate revenue in the short run but the long run sustenance and growth will depend on its ability to harness its manpower and human resources.

The act of 'harnessing human resources', we suggest, is at the core of the concept of learning organization. While defining learning organization Senge (1990) sees 'a group of people continually enhancing their capacity to create what they want to create'. Senge's 'group of people' is not just an amalgam of a few individuals. They work within an organization that provides them the cultural environment conducive to creativity. The cultural environment, following Argyris (1977) and Argyris and Schon (1978), 'may be called an organizational learning system'. A learning organization is, therefore, one that has an effective organizational learning system, or, following Tsang (1997), 'that is good at organizational learning'. Tsang suggests, '... once the definition of organizational learning is settled, that of learning organization will follow.' According to Argyris (1977), organizations learn through individuals acting as agents for them. At the same time it is also recognized that tracing the path of learning organization from individual and organizational learning can be prohibitively complex.

Tsang (1997) reviews the studies that offer some kind of definition of organizational learning. He distinguishes definitions in terms of the perspectives of those studies. Tsang identifies five broad perspectives, namely, cultural, cognitive, cognitive and behavioural (potential), cognitive and behavioural (actual), and behavioural. According to Tsang '... most of the definitions entail aspects of both cognitive and behavioral changes. The cognitive aspect is generally concerned with knowledge, understanding and insights. But there is a split among the definitions on whether a change in actual and potential behavior is required. By potential behavioral change, we mean the lessons learned by an organization would have impact upon its future behavior.' An organization is characterized by its routines. These routines encode and perpetuate lessons learned in the past, and guide the behaviour of an organization. Organizational learning will be reflected in the changes in the routines that will guide the future change in the behaviour of the organization (Levitt and March 1988). Fiol and Lyles (1985), on the other hand, stress improvement in actions through better knowledge and understanding as the process of organizational learning.

We, therefore, look for either changes in the routines or observable change in the behaviour of the organization to know if the organization is learning. Two uncomfortable questions arise here. If 'learning organization is one which is good at organizational learning' (as argued by Tsang 1997), we have to define the extent of changes (potential or actual) that would be considered as good enough to be labeled as learning organization. In the absence of that concept learning organization will remain a riddle devoid of any practical implication. Again, with the definitions used by Tsang we can recognize a learning organization when there are changes at the cognitive level, or in routines, or in behaviour or at all levels. That is at the end of the process of becoming a learning organization. We do not have any clue about the dynamics or the factors that ignited the process of learning in an organization. Such definitions, therefore, offer very little for addressing the issues related to creation of a learning organization or actions necessary for organizational learning.

Miller's (1996) excellent review of literature develops a typology of organizational learning. He tries to locate learning within the axis of Voluntarism – Determinism and Method – Emergence. The first axis spans between autonomous and restricted actions for people in an organization. The other axis varies between intendedly rational actions and actions driven by fad, rituals and normative considerations. Within this axis Miller is able to locate six varieties of modes of learning; three each under the Methodical and Emergent modes. In both the modes, Miller points out, as we move from the Analytical to Experimental to Structural (for the Methodical mode of learning) or from the Synthetic to Interactive to Institutional (for the Emergent mode of learning), the degree of voluntarism decreases. From this typology, Miller could draw quite a few important conclusions. He suggests that with a high degree of voluntarism (few constraints) and within the Analytical and Synthetic modes, learning takes place in the higher echelon of the organizational hierarchy, and diffusion of learning is selective. With lesser voluntarism (action constrained) and within the Experimental and Interactive modes, learning takes place at the middle echelon, and diffusion is narrow. With a still lesser degree of voluntarism (action and thought constrained), which is associated with the Structural and Institutional modes, learning takes place mostly at the lower echelon of the organizational hierarchy, and diffusion is broad based. Miller also suggests the possibility of different modes of learning, and different degrees of voluntarism co-existing in an organization.

Miller's typology helps us in understanding how, when and where in an organization does learning take place. We are, however, still short of building a learning organization. The problem with the definitions and typologies we have discussed above is the absence of a context that motivates an organization to take conscious steps towards building a learning organization. The backdrop of a learning organization is the search for achieving competitive advantage by encouraging an organization to undergo whatever metamorphosis is necessary. In the context of RTOs, as we have already argued in Chapter 4 on 'Effectiveness', achieving competitive advantage means to be ahead of the knowledge base of the clients, and also to have core competence in a niche and specialized area away from the common knowledge. This has close correspondence with the mode 2 of knowledge production articulated by Gibbons *et al.* (1997).[18] It is for achieving competitive advantage that RTOs have to be in pursuit of best practices for transformation into a learning organization. The learning in a learning organization, therefore, is 'transformational learning' (Kofman and Senge 1993). Transformational learning is about changing the mindset of the individual member of an organization towards the fellowship of a community (Vygotsky 1978). It is the process by which external activities are internalized in a new plane of consciousness (Leont'ev 1981). In this process, as Dovey (1997) argues, competitive individualism is replaced by communal learning.

We, therefore, arrive at a different set of questions on what is it that an organization learns, where the learning is stored and how to create a learning organization? Tsang and Miller's reviews do not cover the literature that addresses these questions. A review by Dovey (1997) sets the perspective of learning organization in the context of competitive advantage of capitalist enterprises. Dovey (1997) derives that, 'The ultimate goal of the learning organization is to create a culture of *praxis* within a community characterized by bonded relationship of shared power'. Cultural transformation of an organization takes place through replacement of individualism by fellowship of community. Sharing power and authority is the most difficult but critical ingredient of this transformation (Freire 1974). Once that is achieved the community works as a social group that can collectively explore new learning, solve problems, create new problems, adopt best practices and change forms of organization accordingly. That is the Gramscian concept of *praxis*, of interplay between theory-based action and action-based theory. 'Forms of organization are therefore potentially dynamic' and can be created, sustained and changed through group, community, or social actions (Dovey 1997).

From the above discussion we arrive at the following understanding. We see that a learning organization is not something that happens behind our consciousness. On the contrary, it is to be consciously created in the context of the goal of the organization. Again, adoption of a few best practices within the existing form of an organization is not enough to become a learning organization. It is more regarding creating an organizational culture that ensures a mindset of bonded relationship of a community and power sharing. Learning is consequential to such a cultural environment. Building up such an organization needs actions within. As Dovey observes, 'In all the literature on best practice and learning organizations it is advocated that a "team culture" is the ultimate goal of a learning organization'. Dovey elaborates the role of leadership in initiating the cultural transformation of an organization. He details the virtues and shortcomings of an apprenticeship form as the mode of diffusion of new culture within an organization.

Vigilant organization

At this stage let us reformulate the issues being discussed above. We want an organization to transform in such a way that a process of shared learning is initiated. Such organizations can identify and adopt best practices. In other words, an organization that can identify and adopt best practices is a learning organization. In this understanding of a learning organization there is no trace of a process that leads to its emergence. To trace the process of emergence of a learning organization we have to construct a theoretical relationship between learning ability and the form of an organization. In a form of organization with strict bureaucratic or autocratic control, individuals are answerable for the task he or she has been entrusted with. The dynamics of such an organization is set by the bargaining between individuals and the controlling authority of the organization. The high point of bargaining is to share as little as possible for a return or compensation as high as possible. Clearly, if there is any learning by the individuals of the organization, the learner gains by sharing as little as possible. The process of identification and adoption of best practices, therefore, would be superficial, top down, without conviction and suspect. The process would be further aggravated by the vested interest that enjoys the power and authority from the existing form of the organization. On the other hand, community forms of organizations are expected to be participatory and having more learning ability.

For the present purpose, we shall refrain from any further elaboration of the relationship between learning ability and forms of organizations. Empirical verification of this hypothesis is possible from a socio-anthropological perspective. Our main aim here is to examine a dynamic path for creating a learning organization. Given the relationship between learning ability and forms of organizations, the essential task for the creation of a learning organization is to look for a form of organization that would enhance the learning ability of the organization. The process is gradual and continuous from an autocratic form of an organization to a form of community culture. It is possible to have various forms of organizations in between. The various forms in between would show the characteristics of the co-existence of different modes of learning and different degrees of voluntarism as suggested by Miller. Again, the process is not automatic, and has to be activated with conscious intervention. Who will make such interventions? The leadership of an organization definitely plays a very crucial role. In case the existing leadership is a part of the vested interest of the existing power structure, the process of conscious intervention would be delayed. By definition, therefore, the leadership for change in an organization is possible only when itself is away from the existing power structure.

A vigilant organization is one where the learning ability and the form of organization is monitored and organizational forms are adjusted in favour of enhancing the learning ability of the organization. A learning organization is an outcome of a vigilant organization. But, if learning is a continuous process, sustained learning will be ensured in a vigilant organization.

Notes

1. Based on Alter, P. (1987).
2. Some organizations are scientific-discipline-oriented (for example, Physical Research Laboratory, Chemical Research Laboratory, etc.), some are industry-oriented (for example, Textile Research, Automobile Research, etc.), and some others are technology-oriented (for example, Electronic Research, Biotechnology Research, etc.). In terms of ownership they could be fully owned by the government, or by an industry association, trusts, universities and so on.
3. Araoz (1994) has noted five basic factors underlying growing alienation between RTOs and user industries. These are (1) relative failure to fulfil their original objective of assisting the technological development of industry; (2) a changed milieu with different requirements; (3) a need to update capabilities and develop new skills; (4) an inability to deal with new types of problems; and (5) reduction in state support.
4. For details of processes and sub-processes used in the study, see Grier (1996).
5. It is to be noted here that the sequential steps from scientific research to production are only a stylized presentation of R&D and its applications. In reality, it is concurrent and non-sequential.
6. This section has been developed based on the study, 'Evaluation of Textiles Research Associations of India' undertaken by NISTADS on a research grant from the Ministry of Textiles, Government of India.
7. The study of the evolution of the National Chemical Laboratory, India, has shown how the emphasis on basic research in the initial years of NCL, enabled the laboratory to provide a wide range of technological services to the industry in subsequent years (N. Mrinalini, Nature of R&D and Innovation in a Developing Country: A Study of Pesticides Research in Indian National Laboratories, unpublished PhD thesis, IIT, Delhi).
8. Case of textile research described in Chapter 7. Also see, Nath *et al* (2001).
9. We make a distinction between client and beneficiary. Beneficiaries are those who are being served through RTOs under different promotional and developmental skill of governments. Typical cases are varieties of small industry service organizations and district industry centres (DIC) in India.
10. In a study of Institutes of Research in Textiles (IRTs) it was found that under pressure from the government (the main promoter) for increased generation of revenue, IRTs restructured and reoriented their activities more and more towards physical-resource-based services and training. This essentially meant deploying the existing knowledge base in the revenue-generating mode. The service mix of the IRTs, therefore, has been changed considerably to accommodate those kind of activities where funding is easily available under the various developmental schemes of the government. With such changes in service mix, the IRTs earned much more revenue as compared to earlier years. Industrial R&D, however, took a backseat. And at the time of the study it was observed that the IRTs were facing large-scale attrition of human resources.

The IRTs' manpower with commendable research experience and capability was leaving the IRTs to join the industry for better career and skill development opportunities. This had created a knowledge gap between the IRTs and the industry in favour of the latter, killing the legitimacy of the existence of IRTs.

11. This part of the argument is built up on the basis of the literature on transaction-cost economics. Coase (1937) observed that firms and markets are alternative institutions. Williamson (1975) argued that market failure is the source of transaction cost. Because of asset specificity and bounded rationality, certain transactions have to be executed away from the market. This is the beginning of organization. Transaction cost is the cost incurred for avoiding the market. In Williamson's study it is the undesirable evils of modern market system. Lazonick made a distinction between 'adaptive' enterprise and 'value-creating' enterprise. A firm as an organization, according to Lazonick, tries to gain privileged access to financial, physical and human assets through a widespread vertical and horizontal network. The network is a visible hand and Alchian and Demsetz (1972) described it as the market itself (also see Teubal *et al.* 1991). Through the network, a firm actually internalizes the market within itself. Lazonick argues that when a firm fails in this process of internalization, it takes recourse to trying its luck in the market (Lazonick 1993).

    According to Lazonick, a capitalist enterprise is a value-creating enterprise, the basic dynamic of which is to create a competitive advantage by developing enterprise-specific assets – both physical and human. Transaction cost, however, remains, but it is a cost for developing asset specificity. Lazonick brands a Williamson-type firm as an adaptive enterprise. Further, he makes a distinction between 'market-coordinated' and 'organization-coordinated' enterprises. According to Lazonick, a value-creating enterprise is necessarily 'organization-coordinated' since its basic dynamics is to create asset specificity. On the other hand, an adaptive enterprise is market-coordinated (Lazonick 1993).

    Drawing parallels, an RTO has to develop specific capabilities that will be embodied in its human and physical assets. As an adaptive organization, it will treat its existing assets as given and try to minimize the transaction cost. It will become market-coordinated to derive a price advantage. As a value-creating organization an RTO will create new RTO-specific assets.

12. When an RTO fails to operate in the organization-coordinated mode, it falls back on the market-coordinated mode where it survives on a short-run price advantage offered to its clients in a competitive market for its services. Much of this price advantage is actually derived either from already committed investment on physical resources or subsidized through various government programmes. Such RTOs bank heavily upon equipment- and machine-based service involving minimum human resources. The present state of the Institute of Research in Textiles (IRTs) is an example. After failing to address the client industries' (mainly, spinning, weaving and textile machinery segments) technological needs, IRTs changed their focus to common services like testing and calibration. In doing so, they were competing with a host of other government and non-government agencies offering the same services. The capital investment required for such services was obtained through various types of government support. The IRTs, therefore, did not have to

invest much, and they were able to offer a price advantage to their clients. The IRTs also enjoyed the initial advantage of their earlier goodwill as a research organization. In the meantime, the existing high skilled manpower of IRTs became totally redundant with the change in focus. Most of them left and joined industries. Subsequently, IRTs neither had financial nor human resources for the modernization of services. As a result, they downgraded their services towards low knowledge and low-skill areas, mainly accessing various social upliftment programmes of the government, like short-duration training of tribal youth in weaving with traditional looms and so on. For a detailed analysis of the case, see the Annexure.

13. The case of the Nagoya prefecture in Nath and Mrinalini (1997). See also Ohinishi (1993).

14. In a study on the Institute of Research in Agriculture (IRA) it was found that the IRA was engaging much of its resources for communicating directly with the beneficiaries, and thereby, digressing too far from its core responsibility. In fact, in doing this, the IRA was actually entering a territory that rightfully belonged to its client, in this case the government agency that funded the project. The government has elaborate organizational arrangements for technology transfer to farmers. The organizational effort of the IRA should have been restricted to delivering the total knowledge to these agencies.

    In the case of the Institute of Research in Textiles (IRTs) mentioned earlier, the IRTs were assuming the responsibility of agencies like District Industries Centres (DICs) for imparting primary training in weaving with traditional looms to unemployed rural youths.

    For the ultimate transfer of technology, particularly for rural development and agricultural practices in less developed countries, training and exposing the ultimate beneficiaries to new ways and ideas is very important. The question here is whether the RTOs are the right agencies for performing that task. This is related to the question of the boundary of an organization. The stated objective is better achieved, instead of integrating all vertically and horizontally related activities under one umbrella organization, through a number of organizations, networked with each other, with well-defined and interdependent key functions.

15. In association with Mamata Mondal, who was assisting the authors for the study.

16. Besides the authors, other members of the team that studied the Institute for Research in Textiles are: G. D. Sandhya, S. Visalakshi, P. S. Banerjee and Tabassum Jamal.

17. This chapter is based on Mrinalini and Nath 2000.

18. 'Mode 2 knowledge production is characterised by close interaction between scientific, technological and industrial modes of knowledge production, by the weakening of disciplinary and institutional boundaries, by the emergence of more or less transient clusters of experts, often grouped around large projects of various kinds, and by the broadening of the criteria of quality control and by enhanced social accountability. Secondly, Mode 2 knowledge production is matched on the demand side by the growth of the niche markets for specialised knowledge. This knowledge is obtained by creative configuring and reconfiguring of competence to meet sophisticated user needs.' Gibbons *et al.*, 1997, p. 68.

References

Adler, P. S. and Cole, R. E. (1993) Designed for learning: A tale of two auto plants. *Sloan Management Review* **34**(3): 85–94.

Aiken, M. and Hage, J. (1968) Organizational interdependence and intra-organizational structure. *American Sociological Review* **33**: 912–30.

Alchian, A. A. and Demsetz, H. (1972) Production, information cost, and economic organization. *American Economic Review* **62**: 777–95.

Alter, P. (1987) *The Reluctant Patron, Science and the State in Britain 1850–1920*, trans. by Angela Davies, Oxford: Berg.

Aoki, M. (1986) Horizontal to vertical information structure of the firm. *American Economic Review* **76**(5): 971–83.

Araoz, A. (1994) Revitalization of Technology Research Institutes in Developing Countries, UNIDO, pp. 155–72.

Araoz, A. (1996) 'Revitalization of industrial technology research institutes in developing countries', in M. A. Qureshi (ed.), *Human Resource Needs for Change in R&D Institutes*, New Delhi: WAITRO-NISTADS.

Araoz, A. (1999) Best Practices among Scientific Research Institutes Responding to Strategic Challenges, unpublished project report, IFIAS, Canada.

Argyris, C. (1977) Double loop learning in organizations. *Harvard Business Review*, September–October: 115–25.

Argyris, C. and Schon, D. (1978) *Organizational Learning: A Theory of Action Perspective*, Reading, MA: Addison-Wesley.

Arrow, K. J. (1962a) 'Economic welfare and allocation of resources for innovation', in N. Rosenberg (ed.), *The Economics of Technological Change: Selected Readings*, Harmondsworth: Penguin Books.

Arrow, K. (1962b) The implications of learning by doing. *Review of Economic Studies* **29**: 166–70.

Bell, R. M. (1993) 'Integrating R&D with Industrial Production and Technical Change: Strengthening Linkages and Changing Structures', UNESCO Workshop on Integration of Science and Technology in Development Planning and Management Process.

Bemowaski, K. (1991) The benchmarking bandwagon. *Quality Progress* January, 19–24.

Best, M. H. (1990) *The New Competition Institutions of Industrial Restructuring*, Cambridge, UK: Polity Press.

Boxwell, R. J. (1994) *Benchmarking for Competitive Advantage*, Mcgraw-Hill Inc.

Bush, V. (1945) *Science: The Endless Frontier*, Washington, DC: US Government Printing Office.

Camp, R. C. (1989) *Benchmarking: The Search for Industry Best Practices that Lead to Superior Performance*, Milwaukee: Quality Press.

Coase, R. (1937) Nature of the firm. *Economica* **4**(4): 386–405.

Cheese, J. and Whelan, R. (1996) A process view of technology management – Implications for R&D. *Int. J. Technology Management*, Special Issue on 5th International Forum on Technology Management **11**(3/4): 315–28.

Choo, C. W. (1996) The knowing organization: How organizations use information to construct meaning, create knowledge and make decisions. *International Journal of Information Management* **16**(5): 329–40.

Cohen, W. M. and Levinthal, D. A. (1989) Innovation and learning: The two faces of R&D. *The Economic Journal* 99 (September): 569–96.

Cohen, W. M. and Levinthal, D. A. (1990) Absorptive capacity: A new perspective on learning and innovation. *Administrative Science Quarterly* 35: 128–52.

Dodgson, M. (1993) Organizational learning: A review of some literature. *Organization Studies* **14**(3): 375–94.

Dosi, G. (1988) Sources, procedures and microeconomic effects of innovation. *Journal of Economic Literature* 26: 1120–71.

Dovey, K. (1997) The learning organization and the organization of learning power, transformation and the search for form in learning organization. *Management Learning* **28**(3): 331–49.

Drucker, P. F. (1993) *The Post-capitalist Society*, New York: Harper Collins.

Elzinga, A. and Janison, A. (1995) 'Changing Policy Agenda in Science and Technology', in S. Jasanoff, G. E. Mankle, J. C. Peterson and T. Pinch (eds.), *Handbook of Science and Technology Studies*. Thousand Oaks, California: Sage Publications, pp. 572–97.

Fiol, C. M. and Lyles, M. A. (1985) Organizational learning. *Academy of Management Review* **10**(4): 803–13.

Furukawa, K., Teramoto, Y. and Kanda, M. (1990) Network organization for interfirm R&D activities: Experiences of Japanese small business. *International Journal of Technology Management* **5**(1): 27–40.

Gibbons, M. *et al.* (1994) *The New Production of Knowledge. The Dynamics of Science and Research in Contemporary Societies*, London: Sage Publications.

Gouldner, A. (1959) 'Reciprocity and Autonomy in Functional Theory', in Llewellyn Gross (ed.), *Symposium on Sociological Theory*, New York: Harper and Row.

Gravin, D. A. (1993) Building learning organization. *Harvard Business Review*, July–August, 78–91.

Grier, D. (1996) 'Benchmarking RTOs to Identify Best Practices', in M. A. Qureshi (ed.), *Human Resource Needs for Change in R&D Institutes*, New Delhi: WAITRO-NISTADS, pp. 237–64.

Itoh, M. and Urata, S. (1994) Small and Medium Size Enterprises Support Policies in Japan. WP1403, Policy Research Working Paper, World Bank.

Kee, Y. *et al.* (1994) *Policies and Institutions for Industrial and Technology Development: A Korea Study*, Seoul, Korea: Yonsei University.

Kim, Y., Song, K. and Lee, J. (1993) Determinants of technological innovation in the small firms of Korea. *R&D Management* **23**(3): 215–26.

Kofman, F. and Senge, P. M. (1993) Communities of commitment: The heart of learning organizations. *Organizational Dynamics* **22**(2): 5–23.

Lazonick, W. (1993) *Business Organisation: The Myth of the Market Economy*, New York: Cambridge University Press.

Levitt, B. and March, J. G. (1988) Organizational learning. *Annual Review of Sociology* **14**: 319–40.

Low, M., Nakayama, S. and Yoshioka, H. (1999) *Science Technology and Society in Contemporary Japan*, Cambridge: Cambridge University Press.

Miller, D. (1996) A preliminary typology of organizational learning: Synthesizing the literature. *Journal of Management* **22**(3): 485–505.

Mrinalini, N. (1991) Nature of R&D and Innovation in a Developing Country: A Study of Pesticides Research In Indian National Laboratories. Unpublished PhD thesis, IIT, Delhi.

Mrinalini, N. and Nath, P. (2000) Organizational practices for generating human resources in non-corporate research and technology organization. *Journal of Intellectual Capital* 1(2): 177–86.

Nakayama, S. (1995) 'The Rise of Corporate R&D Activities: The Central Laboratory Boom in Japan', in S. Nakayama, K. Goto and H. Yoshioka (eds.), *The Social History of Science and Technology Contemporary Japan*, Vol. 3, Tokyo, Gakuyo Shobo, pp. 44–9.

Nandi, S. N. (1995) Benchmarking: Principles, Typology and Applications in India. *Productivity* 36(3): 359–70.

Nanjundan, S. (1994) Changing role of small scale industry, international influences, country experiences and lessons for India. *EPW*, xxix(22): M-46–63.

Nath, P. and Mrinalini, N. (1995) Benchmarking of best practices: Case of R&D organization. *Productivity* 36(3): 391–8.

Nath, P. and Mrinalini, N. (1996) Best practices of research and technology organization: Towards a more responsive R&D. *Science, Technology and Society* 1(2): 351–62.

Nath, P. and Mrinalini, N. (1997) Tools for technology assessment: The organizational imperatives. *Asia Pacific Tech Monitor* 14(4): 36–41.

Nath, P. and Mrinalini, N. (2000) Benchmarking the best practices of non-corporate R&D organizations, Benchmarking: *An International Journal* 7(2): 86–97.

Nath, P., Mrinalini, N. and Sandhya, G. D. (2001) National Textile Policy and Textile Research. *EPW*, xxxvi(5&6): 489–96.

Nelson, R. R. and Winter, S. (1982) *An Evolutionary Theory of Economic Change*, Cambridge, MA: Harvard University Press.

Nonaka, I. and Takeuchi, H. (1995) *The Knowledge Creating Company: How Japanese Companies Create the Dynamics of Innovation*, New York: Oxford University Press.

Ohinishi, Y. (1993) Role and Strategies of Public Research Institutes for Small and Medium Enterprises in Japan. Asian Productivity Organization, Tokyo.

Perez-Bustamante, G. (1999) Knowledge management in agile innovative organizations. *Journal of Knowledge Management* 3(1): 6–17.

Piore, M. and Sabel, C. (1984) *The Second Industrial Divide: Possibilities for Prosperity*, New York: Basic Books.

Rosenberg, N. (1976) *Perspective on Technology*, Cambridge: Cambridge University Press.

Rosenberg, N. (1982) *Inside the Black Box*, Cambridge: Cambridge University Press.

Rothwell, R. (1990) External networking and innovation in small and medium sized manufacturing firms in Europe. *Technovation* 11(2): 93–112.

Rothwell, R. and Dodgson, M. (1991) External linkages and innovation in small and medium-sized enterprises. *R&D Management* 21(2): 125–37.

Rush, H., Hobday, M., Bessant, J. and Arnold, E. (1995) Strategies for best practices in research and technology institutes: An overview of a benchmarking exercise. *R&D Management*, 21(1): 17–31.

Senge, P. M. (1990) *The Fifth Discipline: The Art and Practice of the Learning Organization*, London: Century Business.

Simon, H. A. (1957) *Models of Man*, New York: John Wiley.

Simon, H. A. (1976) *Administrative Behaviour: A Study of Decision-making Processes in Administrative Organization*, New York: Free Press.

Singh, D. K. and Evans, R. P. (1993) Effective benchmarking: Taking the effective approach. *Industrial Engineering* 25(2): pp. 22–24.

Slaughter, S. (1993) Beyond basic science. *Science, Technology and Human Values* 18(3): 278–312.

Solow, R. (1957) Technical change and aggregate production function. *Review of Economics and Statistics* 39: 312–20.

Sprow, E. E. (1993) Benchmarking: A tool for our time? *Manufacturing Engineering*, 111(3): 56–69.

Sprow, E. E. (1994) Benchmarking Manufacturing Processes – Your Practical Guide for Becoming Best in the Class. Society of Manufacturing Engineering, Dearborn, Michigan.

SRC (1988) Technology Adoption by Small and Medium Sized Enterprises in Malaysia. Canada.

SRC (1992) Technology Adoption by Small and Medium Sized Enterprises in Singapore. Saskatchewan Research Council, Canada.

Stata, R. (1989) Organizational learning – The key to management innovation. *Sloan Management Review* 30(3): 63–74.

Szakonyi, R. (1994) Measuring R&D effectiveness – I. *Research Technology Management*, March–April: 27–32.

Teubal, M., Yinnon, T. and Zuscovitch, E. (1991) Networks and market creation. *Research Policy* 20: 381–92.

Tsang, Eric W. K. (1997) Organizational learning and the learning organization: A dichotomy between descriptive and prescriptive research. *Human Relations* 50(1): 73–89.

Vygotsky, L. S. (1978) *Mind in Society: The Development of Higher Psychological Processes*, Cambridge, MA: Harvard University Press.

WAITRO (1996) *Best Practices to Strengthen the Capability of Research and Technology Organizations to Facilitate the Development of Small and Medium-sized Enterprises*, Copenhagen, Denmark: WAITRO.

WAITRO (1996) *Strengthening Research and Technology Organization's Capabilities*, unpublished project report, Copenhagen: WAITRO.

Williamson, O. E. (1975) *Markets and Hierarchies: Analysis and Anti-trust Implications*, New York: Free Press.

Ziman, J. (1984) *An Introduction to Science Studies: The Philosophical and Social Aspects of Science and Technology*, Cambridge: Cambridge University Press, pp. 113–19.

Annexure: RTO Processes and Sub-Processes

PROCESSES

1. RTO governance
2. Financial management
3. RTO services
4. Business development
5. Organizational management
6. Project management
7. Capability building
8. Personnel management
9. Networking
10. Policy and programmes

1   RTO Governance

Sub-Processes

1. Ownership
2. Legal structure
3. Constitution of the Board (governing body)
4. Size of the Board
5. Choosing the Board
6. Creation of the RTO's mission and vision
7. Autonomy in key management decisions
8. Mandate
9. Internal decision making
10. Change management process

1.1   Ownership

Defines who legally owns the RTO and is ultimately responsible for it. Ownership is distinct from funding.

Practices	*Number of RTOs*
(a) Fully owned by national government	32
(b) Fully owned by prefecture, province, state, etc. government	10
(c) Fully owned by industry association	4
(d) Not-for-profit foundation, not owned by anyone	9
(e) Several national governments	1

(f) Several provincial governments   1
(g) University   2

Project performance indicators

1. Financial performance
2. Growth in budget or staff
3. Average client income
4. Growth in percentage of client income
5. Assessment of reputation

Observation on best practices: From the industry point of view, *industry specific association owned RTO is considered the best practice*. Weak market forces and inadequate resource mobilization characterize developing countries. In addition to this, SMEs are part of regional development programmes and so the government has to play a critical role in facilitating resource mobilization and creation of a market. In this context, decentralized government ownership structure at *regional/ prefecture/lowest unit of government administration is considered to be the best practice*.

1.2   Legal structure

Defines from whom and how the RTO takes its overall direction.

Project performance indicators

1. Financial performance
2. Growth in budget or staff
3. Average client income
4. Growth in percentage of client income
5. Satisfaction expressed by RTO management

Practices	*Number of RTOs*
(a) *Government Department*: Chief executive is a senior civil servant responsible to government, budgets set by government	4
(b) *Government Agency*: RTO is defined by its own legislation and operates separately from a government ministry, responsible to a minister of the government and a Board that is appointed by the government. Not financially independent of the government	16
(c) *Government Enterprise*: Government owned enterprise, operated independent of the government, responsible to government and government-appointed board, financially independent of the government	14
(d) *Industry Association Agency*: Operates as part of the other operations of the industry association, not financially independent of the association	2
(e) *Industry Association Enterprise*: Operates independently from the industry association with the association providing the governing board and direction	8
(f) *Non-government not-for-profit corporation or foundation*	6

(g) *University enterprise*	1
(h) *Part of university*	2
(i) *Government Foundation Trust not for profit department*	6

Observation on best practice: *Industry association enterprise* is considered to be the best practice in the context of a well-developed industry. In the context of developing countries, where the industry is not in a position to articulate its demand *RTOs under government ownership with functional autonomy* have been generally considered as best practice. The additional criterion suggested for the best practice was the legal status of the RTO, that ensures 'accountability' to the target client. In the context of developing countries where SMEs are generally not in a sound financial position for paying for the best services, 'accountability' to the client's can be ensured through a *'Trust' owned by government constituted of, among others, representatives of target clients*. This is a practice observed in the Japanese Prefecture Laboratories.

1.3   Constitution of the board (governing body)

To have the right set of people on the board that will provide the best direction to the RTO.

Project performance indicators

1. Amount of work with client involvement (percentage of budget from client revenue plus percentage of grant with clients providing project direction – this shows client satisfaction)
2. Growth in staff and/or budget
3. Assessment of services versus mandate
4. Financial goals attained
5. The RTO management satisfied with contribution of board

Practices	*Number of RTOs*
(a) All are government representatives	2
(b) All are industry representatives	4
(c) All are representatives of professional societies	2
(d) All are eminent personalities from the academia and industry	3
(e) Combination of representatives with government having the majority	15
(f) Combination of representatives with industry having the majority	13
(g) Combination of practices (a),(b),(c), with university and research institutions having the majority	5
(h) Fairly balanced representation from government, industry, and university/research institution sectors	11
(i) No external board	5

Observation on best practice: The best practice observed is to have the balanced representation with *target client groups* represented in the board that gives a better perspective of the needs, the available resources and hence a better utilization of the same.

1.4 Size of the board

To have the number of people that is manageable and at the same time functional.

Project performance indicators

1. Amount of work with client involvement (percentage of budget from client revenue plus percentage of grant with clients providing project direction – this shows client satisfaction)
2. Growth in staff and/or budget
3. Assessment of services versus mandate
4. Financial goals attained
5 The RTO management satisfied with contribution of board

Practices	*Number of RTOs*
(a) 6 or less	4
(b) 7 to 10	23
(c) 11–15	6
(d) 16–20	8
(e) >20	2
(f) 6 or less with several smaller committees of the board	1
(g) 11–15 with committees	6
(h) >20 with committees	3
(i) No board	7

Observation on best practice: No specific conclusion in terms of optimum number of persons could be drawn. A suggestion was made in terms of a board having the number of people that is representative of all interested groups and also manageable in terms of participation. This was considered to be appropriate for the smooth and effective functioning of the board.

1.5 Choosing the board

To choose a board that effectively meets the RTO's needs.

Project performance indicators

1. Opinion of management that the board functions well
2. Amount of work with client involvement (percentage of budget from client revenue plus percentage of grant with clients providing project direction – this shows client satisfaction)
3. Assessment of RTO performance relative to mandate and other goals

Practices	*Number of RTOs*
(a) All are appointed by the owner	25
(b) The RTO chief nominates the members, owner accepts or rejects	14
(c) The RTO chief appoints	4
(d) Once constituted, the board itself selects replacements	2

(e) Board members are elected for term by the ownership
(i.e. industry association) or the major client group ... 3
(f) Government and industry together agree on
nominations and appointments ... 1
(g) Groups represented on the board select their
own representatives ... 6
(h) RTO management nominates members, government
(who is *not* the owner) appoints ... 4
(i) No board ... 3

Observation on best practice: *RTO chief's suggestion with owner's approval* is considered to be the best practice. RTO chief would have a better understanding of the RTO's expected performance and with the owner's approval gives scope for owner's intervention.

1.6 Creation of the RTO's mission and vision

To decide and express the RTO's *raison d'être* and its direction for the future.

Project performance indicators

1. The RTO has articulated mission and vision statements
2. Mission and vision statements are updated regularly
3. Mission and vision statements seem to match the services and clients being served

Practices	*Number of RTOs*
(a) The RTO's mission and vision are dictated by the owner	18
(b) The RTO's mission and vision are established by the board through discussions with the owners and the RTO management	4
(c) The RTO's mission and vision are set by its senior management	10
(d) The RTO board alone sets the mission and vision	13
(e) The RTO board approves or modifies proposals from RTO management	6
(f) The RTO board approves or modifies proposals from the RTO that were formed through management and staff discussions	7

Observation on best practice: The board is the best body to have a vision for the RTO. An active board having the right people with client's representation would be in the best position to take decisions regarding the RTO's activities and also the future course of action. The RTO's board approving or modifying a proposal developed through management and staff discussions is considered to be the best practice.

1.7 Autonomy in key management decisions

RTO having autonomy in a way that maximizes its effectiveness (key issues include choice of service mix, target market, staffing decisions, choice of agencies to collaborate with, development of international work, development of resources).

Project performance indicators

1. Opinion of management regarding satisfaction or frustration with system
2. Financial performance
3. Growth in budget or staff
4. Growth in serving clients (growth per cent of client revenue)

Practices	*Number of RTOs*
(a) The RTO is under direct control of a ministry, university or industry association that is responsible for key decisions	11
(b) The RTO is one of many RTOs under an umbrella organization that is responsible for key decisions	2
(c) The RTO board is responsible for most key decisions	9
(d) The RTO has almost full autonomy for making key decisions, but must have a few major ones approved by a higher authority	13
(e) The RTO has full autonomy for all decisions	2
(f) An RTO, which is one of many RTOs under an umbrella organization, has developed considerable autonomy through a client-funded foundation	2
(g) The RTO chief responsible for all key decisions	1

Observation on best practice: Clearly giving the RTO almost full autonomy for making key decisions, with only a few major ones to be approved by the Board or owner, is considered to be the best practice. In developing countries the market itself is undeveloped, and target clients (e.g. SMEs) have to be nurtured for long-term social benefits. In such a situation, the RTO board taking key decisions has been suggested as the best practices since it ensures activities reoriented by the advice of the board constituted of representatives from various interest groups.

1.8 Mandate

To define the RTO's boundaries in terms of geography and/or technology.

Project performance indicators

1. Overall RTO performance

Practices	*Number of RTOs*
(a) *General RTO* mandated to provide technology services in many technology areas to many types of clients in a geographic territory	23

(b) *Technology RTO* mandated to provide specific technology
    services to client groups with a common technology need
    (i.e. paint, industrial engineering, packaging, etc.)   14
(c) *Industry-focused RTO* mandated to provide technology services
    to the clients in an industry group (i.e. fruit processors,
    leather manufacturers, farm machinery manufacturers, etc.)   9
(d) *General-, technology-, or industry-focused RTO* with a
    restricted mandate (such as serving only SMEs or
    indigenous companies)   3
(e) *Multitechnology* multi-industry RTO with national level focus   10

Observation on best practice: It depends upon what the RTO wants to focus upon and so nothing can be specifically said to be best practice. This is essential for the RTO to clearly define its role.

1.9 Internal decision making

To manage the non-project-related day-to-day affairs of the RTO.

Project performance indicators

1. Assessment of staff satisfaction
2. Staff turnover rate
3. Financial performance over 5 years
4. Growth in client revenue
5. Growth in staff and/or budget

Practices   *Number of RTOs*

(a) (*very centralized*) The RTO chief makes almost all internal
    management decisions   13
(b) (*semi-centralized*) The RTO is divided into several divisions
    with the head of those divisions making almost all the
    internal management decisions affecting their division,
    and with other heads and the chief making decisions
    affecting the whole RTO   22
(c) (*semi-decentralized*) The RTO is divided into divisions and
    subdivisions with the head of each subdivision making
    decisions affecting their area and participating in
    division decisions   24
(d) (*decentralized*) The RTO is divided into divisions and
    subdivisions and the individual employees make
    decisions affecting them, and participate with higher
    levels of management as in (b) and (c)   2

Observation on best practice: Most of the RTOs had semi-decentralized practice. This was found to give scope for more participation in decision making at various levels.

1.10 Change management process

To be able to change with changing situations.

Project performance indicators

1. Number of changes and degree of change experienced over its history
2. Growth in staff and/or budget
3. RTO survived the change

Practices	*Number of RTOs*
(a) The RTO has no authority to change with changing situations	8
(b) The RTO's ownership or mandating authority dictates changes required and how the RTO is to incorporate them	10
(c) The RTO board dictates the changes required and how the RTO is to incorporate them	4
(d) The RTO senior management identifies the need for change and proposes changes to board and/or owner and implements them	14
(e) The RTO senior management seeks input from clients, staff, board and owners regarding changes required and how to implement them before making changes	8
(f) The RTO seeks help from outside agency (s) to identify areas for change	5
(g) The Board or advisory committee and owner jointly identify required changes and lead the implementation	8
(h) The RTO owner or mandating authority identifies changes to be incorporated, but the RTO management has freedom to accept or reject them	2

Observation on best practice: In this case, the important aspect for the management is to introduce change with consensus from clients, staff, board and owners. This is considered as the best practice as it takes into account all the related interests.

2   Financial management

Sub-Processes

1. RTO funding methods
2. Government funding (grants) to RTO
3. Methods of establishing amount of grant from owner (government or industry association) (how is it done?)
4. Grant decision making body (who decides on the amount of grant?)
5. Flexibility in use of funds
6. Retention of surpluses and losses from one year to the next
7. Financial management system (FMS)

2.1   RTO funding methods

To acquire the funds necessary to operate the RTO.

Project performance indicators

1. RTO financial performance
2. Growth in budget
3. Percentage of revenue from largest source

Practices	*Number of RTOs*
(a) Majority of funds (>50%) come from government grant	40
(b) Majority of funds (>50%) come from membership fees	1
(c) Majority of funds (>50%) come from contracts	18
(d) Majority of funds come from cess and contracts	1

Observation on best practice: Exact proportion of government support is case specific. It probably works best when RTO's accountability to its clients is ensured by clients' participation in the decision making procedure. Total dependency on government grant brings in the bureaucratic rigidities, curtailing, to a large extent, the operational flexibility in resource development as per the client's requirement. In the case of industry-specific RTOs, and also in the context of developing countries where individual firms in an industry are not capable of mobilizing resources for its own research and technological needs, a 'cess' fund kind of arrangement is suggested as the best practice.

2.2   Government funding (grants) to RTO

To provide the level of support needed to make an RTO viable.

Project performance indicators

1. Overall RTO performance
2. Growth in budget and/or staff
3. Level of grant

Practices	*Number of RTOs*
(a) 100% grant funded	13
(b) 76–99% grant funded	9
(c) 51–75% grant funded	11
(d) 26–50% grant funded	9
(e) 1–25% grant funded	8
(f) 0% grant funded	6

Observation on best practice: As has been observed most of the RTOs get the government grant and as stated earlier the exact proportion is also case specific. Even with 100 per cent government grants there are RTOs that are performing well (Japanese Prefecture Labs). One cannot very specifically say about the grant percentage but the important aspect here is that the RTOs can become more responsive to their clients if their dependency on government grants is reduced. The performance depends on many other factors and so nothing can be clearly stated as the best practice.

2.3   Methods of establishing amount of grant from owner (Government or industry association) (how is it done?)

To establish the amount of the RTO's grant.

Project performance indicators

1. Growth in grant
2. Management comments on effort required
3. Level of grant

Practices	*Number of RTOs*
(a) Does not apply	5
(b) Plan and budget provided by the government or industry association	10
(c) Plan and budget prepared by the RTO and submitted to higher authority who negotiates with the RTO to set the amount	34
(d) Plan and budget submitted by the RTO to higher authority who decides on a budget based on the plan, but without negotiation with the RTO	8
(e) Amount of grant is set by a percentage of industry member sales	2

Observation on best practice: This is also case specific. The government grant can be proportionate to their earnings through service to their clients or through their member industry sales. A government grant is essential for certain basic long-term activities and sustenance of the RTO. This is more so for those RTOs in the developing countries that serve the SMEs, who cannot pay the market price for the services.

2.4   Grant decision making body (who decides on amount of grant?)

To establish the amount of the RTO's grant.

Project performance indicators

1. Growth in grant
2. Management comments on effort required
3. Level of grant

Practices	*Number of RTOs*
(a) Industry association board	4
(b) Government department responsible for RTO	40
(c) Treasury board	5
(d) Parliament or legislature	2
(e) Does not apply	2

Observation on best practice: *Board having representation of the interested groups* can be considered as the best practice for establishing the amount of grant for the RTO.

2.5   Flexibility in use of funds

To use funds in the most effective manner.

Project performance indicators

1. RTO financial performance
2. Growth in RTO budget

Practices	*Number of RTOs*
(a) Fully flexible (money from any source can be used for anything the RTO decides)	5
(b) The RTO has limitations on activities for which grant, membership or cess funds can be used, but has complete flexibility regarding how the money is distributed among things like salary, equipment, travel and so on.	8
(c) The funds from several sources must be kept separate and used only for designated activities although there is flexibility within each fund	3
(d) Grant funds are provided to budget accounts for things like salary, equipment, travel, etc. and cannot be transferred from one account to another (i.e. inflexible), although funds from other sources can be kept separate and used in a flexible manner	10
(e) All the RTO's funds are inflexible because the RTO can either receive funds from sources other than grant or it is forced to use all funds in the same inflexible manner	10
(f) Faced with the inflexibility the RTO uses industry-owned foundations to manage revenue from industry in a way that allows flexibility on that part of its funds	2
(g) Not applicable	2

Observation on best practice: Flexibility in fund utilization is the desirable practice that helps in effective utilization of the fund. This if managed by the board in terms of deciding on areas of its utilization is considered more appropriate.

2.6 Retention of surpluses and losses from one year to the next

This is basically to help the RTO in making financial adjustments for the benefit of the RTO so that the fund is used in the most effective manner.

Project performance indicators

1. Growth in RTO budget
2. Growth in non-grant funds

Practices	*Number of RTOs*
(a) Surpluses in grant or other sources of funds are returned to the owner (government or industry association) each year. The RTO cannot incur losses	31

(b) Surpluses in grant must be returned to the owner
each year, but surpluses in other sources of funds
can be retained in the RTO. The RTO can incur a loss   2
(c) Any surplus or loss incurred by the RTO is retained by the RTO   21
(d) The RTO cannot retain surpluses or losses, but uses
a foundation to manage a portion of its funds to
enable it to retain surpluses in its non-grant revenue   5
(e) Not applicable   2

Observation on best practice: In most of the cases that involve government grant, the RTO is expected to return surplus in the grant and is not expected to make losses. The practice of retaining surpluses is observed mostly in the RTOs in developed countries. This is considered the best practice as it gives the RTO flexibility in financial management.

2.7   Financial management system (FMS)

To provide the information and have necessary controls to facilitate the RTO management to manage its finances and meet its obligations for reporting to its owners and the government.

Project performance indicators

1. Assessment of RTO management and project managers of the capability of their system to meet their needs
2. RTO financial performance

Practices	*Number of RTOs*
(a) The RTO's FMS provides RTO financial information on a quarterly basis	14
(b) The RTO's FMS provides RTO financial information on a monthly basis	4
(c) The RTO's FMS provides RTO and unit information on a monthly basis	1
(d) The RTO's FMS provides RTO, unit and project information on a quarterly basis	1
(e) The RTO's FMS provides RTO, unit and project information on a monthly basis	9
(f) The RTO's FMS provides RTO, unit and project information on a weekly basis	5
(g) The RTO's FMS provides RTO, unit and project information as required (on-line)	6

Observation on best practice: Information management has been the weak point in most of the RTOs in the developing countries. Providing on-line project information is considered the best practice.

3   RTO services

Sub-Processes

1. Service mix
2. Service type
3. Determination of services to be offered
4. Ensuring service quality
5. Role of grant funding in service provided

3.1   Service mix

To provide the mix of services that the target market needs. Types are:

(a) Basic research
(b) Applied research
(c) Experimental development
(d) Consulting
(e) Testing
(f) Training and information dissemination

Project performance indicators

1. Growth in client revenue
2. Evidence of active client interaction with the RTO

Practices	*Number of RTOs*
(a) Concentrate (80 per cent of effort) on one type of service	3
(b) Provides a mix of 3 or 4 to meet needs of clients	17
(c) Provides a mix of 3 or 4 where one is the primary service and the others are offered to attract clients to primary service	6
(d) Provides a mix of 5 or 6 to meet needs of clients	16
(e) Provides a mix of 5 or 6 where one or two are the primary services and the others are offered to attract clients to the primary services	18

Observation on best practice: Providing comprehensive services to the clients is considered to be the best practice wherein, the RTO should try to focus on few primary services and the others are offered to attract clients to primary services. Particularly, in the context of developing countries, where infrastructure available for technological services are not well developed, a single window approach for clients is likely to be more effective.

3.2   Service type

To provide the type of services that the target market needs.

Project performance indicators

1. Growth in client revenue
2. Evidence of active client interaction with the RTO

Practices	*Number of RTOs*
(a) The RTO concentrates (>40% of effort) on basic research	2
(b) The RTO concentrates (>40% of effort) on applied research	26
(c) The RTO concentrates (>40% of effort) on experimental development	6
(d) The RTO concentrates (>40% of effort) on consulting	9
(e) The RTO concentrates (>40% of effort) on testing/quality	11
(f) The RTO concentrates (>40% of effort) on training and information dissemination	1
(g) The RTO does not concentrate on any one type of service	5

Observation on best practice: In the context of developing countries, the main demand of SMEs would be for (e) type of services. The RTO's effectiveness would be proved if these services help SMEs become more competitive in the marketplace and once that happens, the nature of demand for technological inputs from SMEs will also change. The RTO, therefore, in the long run will have to equip itself with higher technological capability to focus on applied research. Therefore, *best* practice is concentrating on applied research if the market and mandate permits.

3.3 Determination of services to be offered

To decide the services that the target market needs.

Project performance indicators

1. Growth in client revenue
2. Evidence of active client interaction with the RTO

Practices	*Number of RTOs*
(a) Mainly based on RTO management's assessment of client needs without formal mechanisms for asking potential clients	13
(b) Mainly based on organized interactions between the RTO and clients where client needs are discussed (*market pull*)	11
(c) Mainly based on market research where clients are consulted about services required (*market pull*)	3
(d) Mainly based on RTO capabilities (*technology push*)	2
(e) Mainly based on owner priority missions (*policy push*)	17
(f) Mainly based on RTO management and researchers' assessment of client needs gleaned from informal contacts with clients and following their technology areas	10

Observation on best practices: For a developed market where clients can articulate their needs, *market research and even organized RTO client interaction* can be considered as the best way of determining the services to be offered. For the market where, clients are to be made aware of their technological needs and potentiality of future market *priority mission oriented services* identified by the board is suggested to be the best practice.

3.4   Ensuring service quality

To ensure that the clients are provided with quality service to their satisfaction.

Project performance indicators

1. Assessment of efforts to control quality
2. Growth in client revenue
3. Evidence of active client interaction with the RTO

Practices	*Number of RTOs*
(a) Free, subsidized or statutory required services so clients accept quality provided and RTO makes no effort to ensure quality	19
(b) Clients pay for services so it is assumed that if quality is poor, clients won't pay	1
(c) Clients receive regular client satisfaction surveys inquiring about the quality of the service	9
(d) Regular organized interactions with clients where quality issues are discussed	14
(e) Some RTO services are certified under a recognized quality programme	6
(f) All services and/or the RTO is certified under a recognized quality programme	4
(g) Demonstration of results before clients have to accept them	8
(h) Follow-up visits with clients after project conclusion to discuss results	13
(i) Clients participate with RTO staff on projects	5
(j) RTO has internal committee to manage project quality	2

Observation on best practice: *Organized interaction with clients and getting their feed on service quality*, on a regular basis, is considered to be the best practice.

3.5   Role of grant funding in service provided

To use grant funding to support services provided by the RTO.

Project performance indicators

1. RTO financial performance
2. Percentage of effort with client
3. Growth in client revenue
4. Assessment of satisfaction with use of grant

Practices	*Number of RTOs*
(a) No grant funding available	1
(b) Grant funding applied to support administration, marketing, facilities, etc.	8
(c) Grant funding applied to support all service types in the same proportion as client revenue	4
(d) Grant funding used mainly for capability building	4

(e) Grant funding used mainly to support basic research	5
(f) Grant funding used mainly to support applied research	1
(g) Grant funding used mainly to support experimental development	1
(h) Grant funding used mainly to support consulting	1
(i) Grant funding used mainly to support training and information dissemination work	1
(j) Grant funding supports > 90% of the RTO's activities	13

Observation on best practice: It appears that utilizing grant fund to the RTO's service areas in proportion to the revenue from those areas is considered the best practice. In addition, utilizing grant for building capability by taking up basic research is again considered to be very useful for the RTOs to work out projects in futuristic areas.

4 Business development

Sub-Processes

1. Management of business development – allocation of responsibilities
2. Rewards for business development successes
3. Financing business development activities
4. Awareness creation strategy
5. Identification of client group needs
6. Identification of individual client needs
7. Project pricing methods
8. Methods for reducing the cost of projects to clients (leveraging)

4.1 Management of business development – allocation of responsibilities

To coordinate and conduct business development activities as effectively (bringing in enough business) and efficiently (lowest cost) as possible.

Project performance indicators

(a) Financial performance of RTO (Is there enough business to meet costs?)
(b) Percentage of client revenue
(c) Growth in client revenue
(d) Business development cost over revenue
(e) Growth in number of clients

Practices	*Number of RTOs*
(a) The chief executive conducts or directs all strategic market planning, awareness creation, client interaction, proposal writing and contract negotiation	16
(b) The division manager conducts the activities described in (a) for his division while the chief does awareness creation and planning at the RTO level	11
(c) The RTO has a corporate business development group that conducts the activities described in (a)	12

(d) The RTO has a corporate business development group
that conducts awareness creation and supports senior
management in market planning while activities related to
specific projects (proposals, client interaction, contracts, and
some awareness creation) are conducted by the division manager   8
(e) Same as (d) except that individual project managers
conduct the division manager activities   11
(f) External agencies are appointed for undertaking business
development activity   2

Observation on best practice: It is considered as best practice to have a separate
marketing division with special emphasis on orientation of RTO's staff on business development through internal and external training programmes.

4.2   Rewards for business development successes

To encourage staff to contribute more towards growth in client revenue.

Project performance indicators

1. Percentage of client revenue
2. Growth in client revenue
3. Business development cost over client revenue
4. Growth in number of clients

Although, information on (3) & (4) are sometimes not available.

Practices	*Number of RTOs*
(a) Business development is not specifically encouraged	30
(b) Managers or project managers that develop more business are given more recognition, prestige and perks (i.e. conference travel budgets)	13
(c) Performance management systems include meeting client revenue targets as a significant objective resulting in those that do well in this area getting higher increases and bonuses	5
(d) Those responsible for sales are given the majority of their income through sales commissions and have almost no income without sales	1
(e) Professionals share revenues in excess of the RTO's cost	11

Observation on best practice: In most of the RTOs in the developing countries
there is no special recognition for business development. In order to encourage
and enthuse people to contribute more towards business development, it is
considered as the best practice to show recognition through rewards.

4.3   Financing business development activities

To manage the cost of business development while ensuring proper business
development activities.

Project performance indicators

1. Percentage of client revenue
2. Growth in client revenue
3. Business development cost over client revenue
4. Growth in number of clients
5. Assessment of business development activities

(3) and (4) are sometimes not available.

Practices	*Number of RTOs*
(a) All business development costs are absorbed in operating costs and therefore are not budgeted or tracked	27
(b) A centrally-controlled business development budget is created and all costs are charged against the budget	4
(c) Corporate business development activities (like planning, awareness creation) have a budget that is controlled centrally while those in the operating units must fund their activities out of project money	22
(d) Corporate personnel and those at the unit level have business development budgets and track cost against them	5

Observation on best practice: Having a separate budget is a good practice for the simple reason that a planned publicity programme is possible on the basis of available resources. The best practice appears to be a *centralized publicity campaign*. It is seen as having advantages similar to 'brand' development by creating an image of the RTO.

4.4 Awareness creation strategy

To inform those who are to be the recipients of the RTO's services and those who fund the RTO for its capabilities, services and successes.

Project performance indicators

1. Assessment of amount and quality of awareness activities
2. Percentage of client revenue
3. Growth in client revenue
4. Business development cost over client revenue

Practices	*Number of RTOs*
A. Primarily conducts awareness activities that focus on reaching the public for influencing the funders:	
1. news releases	23
2. advertising in media	10
3. public meetings	2
4. hosting public tours	2
5. radio/TV programmes	7

B. Primarily conducts awareness that focuses on major client group(s):

1. industry newsletter	14
2. host industry seminars	26
3. project plan meetings	12
4. industry tours of RTO	24
5. RTO tours of companies	22
6. RTO booth in trade show	19
7. mail brochures to companies	17
8. publish in industry journals	13
9. advertise in industry journals	8
10. join industry associations	7
11. sell RTO memberships	7
12. international reputation	12

C. Primarily conducts awareness that focuses on individual companies in a territory:

1. mail brochures, letters	13
2. visit companies	13
3. invite companies to the RTO	11
4. telephone promotion	1
5. mail newspaper, magazine	8
6. booth at territorial shows	6
7. lobby with industry associations	7

D. Conducts awareness that focuses on funder:

1. put on board	17
2. communicate successes	20
3. gather testimonials	18
4. propose new initiatives	19

E. Conducts awareness that focuses on developing an international reputation for being an expert in a field:

1. host international meetings	13
2. publish in international journals	16
3. advertise on Internet	9
4. project with international expert	13
5. speak/publish internationally	14
6. do international projects	20
7. promote work with MNCs	16
8. serve on international organizations	8

Observation on best practice: Here all the practices are good. The most important unique practice, generally found among prefecture laboratories of Japan, is 'free on site consultancy'. This builds up not only strong interaction with the firms/industries but also the confidence of clients on the RTO. Another unique practice is found in one of the RTOs, where funders and clients are in the decision making board.

4.5 Identification of client group needs

To identify client needs in order to decide what services the RTO should offer.

Project performance indicators

1. Assessment of growth in services offered
2. Assessment of services offered versus likely needs of clients being served
3. Growth in client revenue
4. Client interaction

Practices	*Number of RTOs*
(a) Identification of client needs and to whom it is mandated by outside forces (i.e. government) so the RTO does not try to identify needs	2
(b) Identification of client needs is mainly decided by the senior management based on personal knowledge of the clients being served and the technologies needed to serve those clients	7
(c) Identification of client needs is mainly decided by engineers and scientists in the RTO based on personal knowledge of the clients and the technologies needed to serve those clients	8
(d) Identification of client needs is mainly decided by senior management based on input from the RTO's scientists and engineers	11
(e) Identification of client needs is mainly decided by senior management based on input from the RTO's scientists and engineers, and from board members from the industry	9
(f) Identification of client needs is mainly decided by senior management based on input from RTO personnel, board members, regular meetings with industry	12
(g) Identification of client needs is mainly decided by senior management based on input from RTO personnel, board members, regular meetings with industry and surveys (market research)	5
(h) Types of services offered is mainly decided by the board represented by clients, academia, government and RTO senior management	6

Observation on best practice: Identification of client needs by management based on input from RTO staff, board members and regular meetings with industry is by far the *best* practice. Having representation of clients in the Board, which makes decision about client group's need, has real potentiality for building up a long-term interest of clients in the RTO. In fact, RTOs in that case become a part of the clients and vice versa.

4.6 Identification of individual client needs

To identify individual client needs.

Project performance indicators

1. Growth in client revenue
2. Client interaction

Practices	*Number of RTOs*
(a) Relies on clients to come to RTO with needs	3
(b) Reaches out to clients in 1 to 3 ways	19
(c) Reaches out to clients in 4 to 6 ways	13
(d) Reaches out to clients in 7 to 10 ways	5

Observation on best practice: Not reaching out to clients is the bad practice. Any way of reaching out to the clients is considered to be a good practice. We have come across certain unique ways of reaching out to clients like, providing *free on site consultancy* to individual clients, *to organize and or deliver technology clinics and seminars* and to offer a *subscription programme* by which, the services to the subscribers are subsidized.

4.7   Project pricing methods

To set the price for the work done for clients in a way that enables the RTO to best meet its financial targets.

Project performance indicators

1. RTO financial performance
2. Percentage client revenue
3. Growth in client revenue
4. Marketing costs divided by client revenue

Practices	*Number of RTOs*
(a) Services are free, nominal charge for use of facilities	2
(b) RTO's client revenue is mainly from projects that are acquired through the writing of a proposal describing the work, cost, deliverables and schedules which form the basis for a contract between the RTO and the client	23
(c) Standard services provided at subsidized rate	2
(d) The RTO uses (b) for some services and standard services for others	14
(e) As in (d), with standard services being subsidized and projects priced according to a formula	14
(f) The RTO uses market- or value-based pricing to establish the price for its pre-priced services	4
(g) The RTO uses market- or value-based pricing to establish the price for its pre-priced services	3

Observation on best practice: It has been generally agreed upon that from a developing country's perspective subsidized technical services to SMEs have to be there. Experts think that the real issue is management of subsidy so that the subsidy goes to the right target client and withdrawal of subsidy is rightly timed. Market-based pricing to be set for the pre-priced services can be considered the best practice in the context of developed countries where the firms can afford to pay the market price for the services and are in a position to articulate their demands.

4.8 Methods for reducing the cost of projects to clients (leveraging)

To enable clients to acquire RTO services at a price they can afford while providing the RTO adequate revenue.

Project performance indicators

1. Assessment of RTO success related to leveraged projects
2. RTO financial performance
3. Growth in industry revenue
4. Client revenue/total revenue
5. Cost of marketing divided by total revenue

Practices	*Number of RTOs*
(a) The RTO is heavily funded resulting in considerable leveraging by default	18
(b) The RTO is mainly funded through a grant and/or industry memberships and the RTO submits proposals to industry committees proposing projects for their approval	5
(c) The RTO levers mainly with government programmes to assist in funding its projects and writes proposals to the programmes and clients in a manner that helps the client get money from the programme	4
(d) The RTO levers mainly with grant funding	2
(e) The RTO levers mainly with grant and government programme money and consortium of clients to make projects affordable to clients	5
(f) The RTO does very little levering	6

Observation on best practice: Government grant money can be used to help those firms which cannot afford market rate and at the same time need the services of the RTO. The board can decide this. This is observed in most of the RTOs in developing countries where service to SMEs is provided free of cost or at highly subsidized rates.

5 Organizational management

Sub-Processes

1. Organizational management style
2. Grouping of RTO capabilities
3. Organizational unit responsibility level

5.1 Organizational management style

To provide the support, supervision, direction setting, and communication to employees so that the RTO is able to meet its goals.

Project performance indicators

1. RTO financial performance
2. Growth in client revenue
3. Growth in staff or budget
4. Assessment of how well RTO meets client needs (client interaction)

Practices	*Number of RTOs*
(a) *'Family':* hierarchical, central, person oriented, informal relationships, status given by father figure, management by subjectives	12
(b) *'Eiffel Tower':* hierarchical, central, task oriented, formal relationships, status by ascription, management by job description	6
(c) *'Guided Missile':* decentral, equality, task oriented, informal relationships, status by accomplishments, management by objectives	18
(d) *'Incubator':* decentral, equality, person oriented, informal relationships, status by accomplishing creativity, management by enthusiasm	2

Observation on best practice: Eiffel tower management practice is not considered good. In other practices there is interaction, scope for exchange of views and so decisions can be on the basis of consensus. This helps in smooth functioning of the RTO because of open communication channel.

5.2 Grouping of RTO capabilities

To structure the staff into groups that allows the RTO to meet its goals most efficiently.

Project performance indicators

1. RTO financial performance
2. Growth in client revenue
3. Growth in staff or budget
4. Assessment of how well RTO meets client needs (client interaction)

Practices	*Number of RTOs*
(a) RTO is divided into units based on *technology* (electronics, computers, mechanical engineering, biotechnology, etc.)	28
(b) RTO is divided into units focused on *industry sectors* (wood products, plastics processors, agriculture, metals, etc.)	3
(c) The RTO is divided into units based on *type of service* (research, consulting, testing, training, etc.)	10
(d) RTO uses a combination of the above methods to form individual units	17

Observation on best practice: Departmentalization in the academic discipline line or industry line is no longer practised in most of the RTOs. It is felt that the organization responsible for undertaking industrial research and technological services for a targeted client group should organize its manpower accordingly. Divisions in academic lines confuse the purpose of the organization. Furthermore, a division in the line of technology or services, or a combination of the two can provide more comprehensive service to the client. The general opinion is that RTOs organized in technology or service line is the best practice.

5.3 Organizational unit responsibility level

To give the unit the level of responsibility that results in the best RTO performance.

Project performance indicators

1. Assessment of RTO relationship with clients
2. RTO financial performance
3. Percentage of projects delivered on time
4. Percentage of projects delivered on budget

Practices	*Number of RTOs*
(a) Responsible for providing good technical results (activity centre, responsible for doing the activity well)	6
(b) Responsible for providing good technical results within cost and time constraints provided by someone outside the unit (cost centre, responsible for doing the activity well and managing costs)	5
(c) Responsible for providing good technical results according to contract arrangements made within the unit (profit centre, responsible for doing the activity well, managing cost and revenue)	9

Observation on best practice: Giving the unit full responsibility for financial performance (revenue and costs), while expecting high-quality technical results, is the *best* practice.

6 Project management

Sub-Processes

1. Project management structure
2. Functional authority for project management
3. Grant funded project selection
4. Project assignment
5. Contract signing authority
6. Project management method
7. Project follow-up

6.1 Project management structure

To create a team that most effectively and efficiently does RTO's projects.

Project performance indicators

1. Assessment of quality of RTO's work
2. Growth in client revenue
3. RTO financial performance
4. Assessment of client satisfaction (client interaction)

Practices	*Number of RTOs*
(a) Project teams are formed from the people in the unit doing the project	4
(b) Project teams are mainly formed from the people in the unit doing the project with people from other units used when special expertise is needed	13
(c) Project teams are mainly formed with appropriate personnel gathered from a number of units	3

Observation on best practice: In most of the cases, a team is formed depending on the need of a project. Therefore, all three practices are prevalent in the RTOs studied. The *best* practice is to form project teams with appropriate personnel gathered from a number of units

6.2   Functional authority for project management

To direct the project activities in a manner that results in a successful project.

Project performance indicators

1. Assessment of processes used to manage projects
2. Growth in staff or budget
3. RTO financial performance
4. Assessment of involvement with clients

Practices	*Number of RTOs*
(a) The RTO chief manages all projects	1
(b) The heads of all major departments manage all projects being done in their department	19
(c) The heads of sub-departments manage all projects being done in their sub-department	2
(d) The project leaders are given the responsibility and authority to manage projects within a rigid structure of rules and approvals	26
(e) The project leaders have the authority and responsibility to manage projects without interference once the project plan has been thoroughly checked and approved by the management; changes in project plans require formal revision and re-approval	4
(f) Individual project leaders have authority and responsibility to manage projects with only loose guidelines provided by the RTO's management	8

Observation on best practice: Decentralization of authority is generally considered to be conducive to quick decision making and efficient functioning. It also helps develop the next generation of leadership. From this point of view *delegation of authority at the project leader level* is considered the best practice. However, it has also been argued that there could be misuse of authority if there are no proper counter checks. Authority, therefore, has to go along with accountability. It is, therefore, suggested that with delegation of authority, project leaders also have to be made fully responsible for the outcome of the project. The *best* practice is to give project leaders authority and responsibility to manage projects without interference once the project has been thoroughly checked and approved by management.

6.3   Grant funded project selection

To decide what projects to do that will use the RTO's grant funds in a manner that meets the RTO's goals.

Project performance indicators

1. Assessment of use of grant funds relative to RTO's goals
2. Involvement of RTO with client/beneficiaries
3. Growth in client revenue

Practices	*Number of RTOs*
(a) Governing body selects projects	14
(b) Separate advisory committee selects projects	11
(c) Committee of industry and RTO experts decide what projects to be done	3
(d) The RTO chief selects projects to be done	3
(e) Major department heads select projects	11
(f) A committee of RTI managers decide what projects to do	6
(g) A committee of RTO managers and project leaders decide what projects to do	1
(h) A committee of leading technical experts at the RTO decides on proposals submitted by project leaders	3
(i) Each unit head decides what to do with the portion of grant allocated to him/her after consultation with his/her project manager	4

Observation on best practice: A separate advisory committee or the board selecting the project is the best practice. It has been suggested that the board having the authority to select projects can dovetail activities of the RTO along the line of mandate and mission. The ideal is to have a board where relevant interests groups are represented and entrusted with deciding the activities of the RTO.

6.4   Project assignment

To select the person(s) to conduct projects so that the RTO's goals are met.

Project performance indicators

1. Assessment of RTO involvement with clients/beneficiaries
2. Growth in client revenue
3. RTO financial performance

Practices	*Number of RTOs*
(a) The *RTO chief* selects person(s) to conduct projects	4
(b) The *major department head* is always the project manager	10
(c) The *Major department head selects* person (s) to conduct projects	23
(d) The *Sub-department manager selects* person(s) to conduct projects	6
(e) *A separate committee selects* the person(s) to conduct projects	2
(f) *Individuals* at all levels are responsible for interacting with clients, formulating projects and in effect select themselves to conduct the projects they do	12

Observation on best practice: Individuals at all levels being responsible for interacting with clients, formulating projects and, in effect, selecting themselves as project leaders is the *best* practice. Both (c) and (f) are good practices. In (c) the divisional head having a better idea about the capability of staff of the division would be in a position to select the leader depending on the requirement. In (f) as the project is formulated by the concerned scientist/engineer, he would be the best person to be the leader. However, (f) is not a common practice, and in most of the cases, it is the department manager who is entrusted with the formulation of a project and/or has credibility with clients. In that sense both (c) and (f) become the same practice.

6.5   Contract signing authority

To give commitment on behalf of the RTO for performing work according to the agreement with the client.

1. RTO financial performance

Project performance indicators

1. RTO financial performance
2. Growth in client revenue
3. Assessment of the RTO management's satisfaction with process

Practices	*Number of RTOs*
(a) The RTO chief reviews and signs all contracts	36
(b) The Major department head reviews and signs contracts with that department	7
(c) Two signatures are required on all contracts	1
(d) The level of the person signing the contract depends on the size of the contract	7
(e) The RTO has a contract office that manages and signs all contracts	4
(f) An authority outside the RTO signs all contracts	3

Observation on best practice: Having a contracts office to handle all contracts is a practice that may reduce various steps and procedures and speed up the process. This is not the common practice. Especially in the developing countries, except for two RTOs, this authority is generally vested with the RTO chiefs. For small sized Prefecture Laboratories of Japan it does not make much of a difference.

It has been viewed that this practice generally causes administrative delays but for a general coherence of the RTOs' activities, the practice is generally preferred to other practices. It is also viewed that clients generally feel confident if the contract has the endorsement of the RTO chief.

6.6   Project management method

To keep the project on time and within the budget.

Project performance indicators

1. Assessment of project management process
2. RTO financial performance
3. Growth in client revenue
4. Percentage client revenue

Practices	*Number of RTOs*
(a) Informal, little effort is spent to manage the project's budget or schedule	2
(b) Progress of the project in terms of the project's goals only is estimated and reported by the project leader	19
(c) Progress of the project in terms of the goals and time schedule is estimated and reported by the project leader	13
(d) Progress of the project in terms of the goals is estimated and the costs are monitored by a project accounting system and reported by the project leader	6
(e) Progress of the project in terms of the goals is estimated, time schedule is evaluated against project milestones, and costs are monitored by a project accounting system and reported by the project leader	9
(f) Computerized project management tools are used to monitor progress in terms of goals, time and costs	2
(g) Separate cell does project monitoring in terms of time and cost	3
(h) Separate committee does project monitoring in terms of time and cost	2

Observation on best practice: The general consensus is that monitoring should be the responsibility of the project leader. This also is the common practice among the RTOs covered. At the same time, experts also feel that there has to be a systematic project-based information system to provide the project leader with required information on cost, time and budget. Having a system that monitors budget costs and milestones and requires the project manager to report progress of results, expenditure and timeliness relative to the plan is the *best* practice.

6.7   Project follow-up

To ensure the client is satisfied with completed work and to explore opportunities for future work.

Project performance indicators

1. Assessment of client used
2. Growth in client revenue
3. Level of repeat business

Practices	*Number of RTOs*
(a) No follow-up is done	10
(b) Informal, unplanned interaction with clients	9
(c) Client feedback forms sent out after every project (or clients are phoned by a person not involved in the project to check on satisfaction)	4
(d) Meetings with clients are held after the end of every project	7
(e) Regular meetings are held to continually review results of past work and to plan future projects	19
(f) A combination of client satisfaction survey and follow-up meetings are used	5

Observation on best practice: All the RTOs have a mix of formal and informal follow-up practices. Having a formal system of getting regular feedback from clients and to review past work and plan future work based on the feedback and regular meetings with clients is considered to be the best practice.

7   Capability-building

Sub-Processes

1. Identification of the decision to acquire capability-building opportunities – who does it?
2. Identification of capability-building opportunities – how is it done?
3. Method of funding staff improvement.
4. Method of funding capital investments that improve capabilities.

7.1   Identification of the decision to acquire capability-building opportunities – who does it?

To identify the need for developing new skills or acquiring new staff, equipment or technology to address client needs and opportunities.

Project performance indicators

1. Assessment of how current the RTO is in appropriate technology
2. Growth in client revenue
3. Client interaction

Practices	*Number of RTOs*
(a) The governing body outside the RTO identifies opportunities and decides which to acquire	19
(b) The RTO chief identifies opportunities and decides which to acquire	5

(c) A committee of internal experts (management and staff)
identifies opportunities and decides which to acquire · 4
(d) Individual scientists identify opportunities and submit them
to management for decision · 10
(e) A combination of sources (board, external committee,
internal committee, management and employees) are used
to identify opportunities and management decides
which to acquire · 15
(f) Division/department heads suggest areas of capability building · 5
(g) Management division through industry survey · 2

Observation on best practice: In general, an active governing body/advisory committee with substantial say of the users of RTO services should play a role to identify the areas of capability building. However, the thrust remains on a regular survey of users' need for planning the areas of capability building. Hence, the *best* practice is the one where the management decides on capability opportunities after acquiring input from external and internal boards/committees and individual managers and staff.

7.2   Identification of capability-building opportunities – how is it done?

To identify the need for developing new skills or acquiring new staff, equipment or technology to address client needs and opportunities.

Project performance indicators

1. Assessment of how current the RTO is in appropriate technology
2. Growth in client revenue
3. Client interaction

Practices	*Number of RTOs*
(a) The views of an external group (governing body, committee of clients and experts) are accepted	13
(b) The RTO management consults with a network of clients and technology experts in an informal fashion	1
(c) The RTO uses a combination of informal opportunity identification methods	18
(d) The RTO makes a concerted, formal effort to identify opportunities that collects data in a formal fashion from technology experts and clients	8

Observation on best practice: The *best* practice is to make concerted formal effort to identify opportunities for capability building. A board or a governing body having the client's representation would be in a better position to identify the opportunities for capability building.

7.3   Method of funding staff improvement

To undertake and fund activities that will build staff capability.

Project performance indicators

1. Assessment of amount and type of training being acquired by staff
2. Growth in client revenue
3. Assessment of RTO involvement with clients
4. Percentage of budget spent on training

Practices	*Number of RTOs*
(a) The RTO does not encourage staff capability-building; anything that is done, is done on an individual's own time and at his own expense	1
(b) Uses one method of funding staff improvement	1
(c) Uses two methods of funding staff improvement	11
(d) Uses three methods of funding staff improvement	20
(e) Uses four methods of funding staff improvement	15
(f) Uses five or more methods of funding staff improvement	12

Observation on best practice: The general opinion is that all these practices are good practices except for the first one. In fact, it was suggested that the best practice is a combination of all the above practices depending upon the resource mobilization capability of the RTO.

7.4   Method of funding capital investments that improve capabilities

To acquire the equipment needed to deliver appropriate services to the clients.

Project performance indicators

1. Assessment of RTO involvement with clients
2. Growth in client revenue
3. Assessment of RTO's technology
4. Percentage of budget spent on training

Practices	*Number of RTOs*
(a) The RTO submits requests and justifications to its governing/funding body for capital purchases	7
(b) The RTO receives a portion of its grant dedicated to capital purchases	17
(c) The RTO applies to external programmes like international development agencies or national programmes for loans or grants to pay for capital improvements	18
(d) The RTO funds capital improvements out of its operating budget	6
(e) The RTO acquires equipment donations or loans from manufacturers and/or donations or bequeaths of money from outsiders to fund capital improvements	3
(f) The RTO acquires projects that entail acquisition of capital equipment from clients and/or government agencies	13
(g) Creates fund for capital investment from surpluses	8

(h) Creates client-owned foundation or company to fund
   capital improvements   4
(i) A portion of the industry cess fund is used to fund capital
   equipment at the RTO   2

Observation on best practice: Both (g) and (i) are good practices for resource development. In (g) the RTO enjoys the flexibility for its capital equipment development on the basis of the client's demand. It helps closer interaction with clients.
RTOs which are totally dependent on government for funding and also those
which are not expected to generate revenue, do not have the option of practice
(g) and hence in this case funding for capital equipment has to be through
annual budget or through projects from external agencies. This no doubt, would
curtail their flexibility in using the fund as per client requirement. Practice (i)
ensures developing the facility on the basis of clients' demand.

8 Personnel management

Sub-Processes

1. Recruitment/hiring
2. Appointment of staff to supervisor/managerial positions
3. Advancement of technical staff
4. Compensation
5. Compensation package decision making
6. Non-pay based rewards
7. Staff evaluation
8. Discharging staff
9. Internal communications

8.1 Recruitment/hiring

To acquire the staff with the expertise required to meet the RTO's needs.

Project performance indicators

1. Assessment of satisfaction with present process
2. Growth in client revenue
3. Growth in staff
4. Average percentage hired/year

Practices   *Number of RTOs*

(a) The RTO does not have autonomy in recruitment
   and therefore has no process (staff are assigned to it)   24
(b) The RTO uses an informal process of recruitment,
   hiring from an existing pool of people that it knows,
   with the RTO chief and other management personnel
   making the hiring decision together   1
(c) The RTO uses a formal but flexible process of advertising
   internally and externally, interviewing and selection by
   management   2

(d) The RTO uses a formal but flexible process of advertising
internally and externally, interviewing and selection by a
team of management, coworkers and the HR department   18
(e) The RTO has a formal, inflexible, time-consuming process that
causes it to seldom use it and to contract temporary employees
to meet needs   12
(f) Although the RTO has a useful recruitment process, it is
prevented from using it by its governing body (i.e. hiring
freeze) and so has developed a method of acquiring staff
through an associated, client-funded foundation to meet needs 4

Observation on best practice: In many of the developed countries RTOs have a
formal flexible process that uses input from managers, coworkers and human
resource experts to select new hands which is also considered to be the best
practice. The common practice that one came across in most of the RTOs that are
under government ownership, is that there are rigid rules for both hiring and
discharging of regular employees. It is generally agreed upon that a practice in
this context is mainly dependent on the socioeconomic and political environment of a country. Allowing for these constraints, a best practice appears to have
flexibility in recruiting people on a contract basis as and when required.

8.2   Appointment of staff to supervisor/managerial positions

To have the most appropriate persons in supervisory/managerial positions.

Project performance indicators

1. Assessment of satisfaction with process used
2. Overall RTO performance

Practices   *Number of RTOs*

(a) Appointments are granted by a body, outside the RTO   2
(b) RTO management team decides appointments based on
their impression of the performance and worth of the individual 5
(c) Appointments to positions are handled with the same
advertisement and interview process as external recruitment
with the immediate supervisor of the position making
the decision   2
(d) Appointments to positions are handled with the same
advertisement and interview process as external recruitment
with a team of affected people involved in the decision   11

Observation on best practice: In the developing countries most of the RTOs did
not have any separate managerial or supervisory position and this is observed in
the developed countries. It has been found that recruitment through a selection
process by a team is considered to be the best practice as it offers scope for getting
good people from outside as well. Even promoting people to a higher grade, by
the management, based on their assessment is considered to be the best practice
in smaller RTOs where the management can have direct interaction with the staff.

8.3   Advancement of technical staff

To advance/promote technical staff within their technical/professional stream.

Project performance indicators

1. Assessment of satisfaction with process used
2. Overall RTO performance

Practices	*Number of RTOs*
(a) Advancement within technical/professional stream is not possible	1
(b) No promotion, citation from the RTO chief for best performance	5
(c) Advancement from one technical/professional level to another is automatic based on years of service and qualifications (time bound)	5
(d) Advancement from one technical/professional level to another is fairly automatic; however, the individual's annual performance impacts the rate at which he/she advances (time bound and evaluations)	7
(e) Advancement from one technical professional level to another is entirely based on results of the performance management system	14
(f) Advancement from one technical professional level to another is decided by the RTO chief or supervisor independent of professional management and years of service	1
(g) Advancement from one technical/professional level to another is decided by a committee of peers independent of performance management and years of service	1
(h) All jobs are posted, anybody can apply, formal selection process	4
(i) A percentage of the posts are kept for internal promotion, the rest are open	1

Observation on best practice: Basing advancement from one technical/professional level to another on the results of the performance evaluation by the management system is considered to be the best practice in the context of the North American RTOs. In the Asian subcontinent, it is interesting to observe that except in 13 of the 20 RTOs that we studied, there is no promotional reward for employees. Practice of *in situ* promotion, although might provide great material incentive to the employees, closes the door to external competition with the risk of heavy inbreeding. Practice (i) is unique where a percentage of vacant positions are kept for internal promotion and the rest are open for external competition. This practice helps in getting new people and at the same time gives opportunity to the existing staff to compete through their performance.

8.4   Compensation

To compensate employees for their contribution to the RTO, to encourage high performance, and to attract appropriate talent.

Project performance indicators

1. Assessment of package used
2. Overall RTO performance

Practices	Number of RTOs
(a) RTO salaries are rigid and are set according to a formula; salaries are equal to or better than could be acquired in industry	1
(b) RTO salaries are rigid and are set according to a formula similar to government employees; salaries are lower than could be acquired in industry	28
(c) RTO salaries are rigid and are set according to a formula better than government but lower than industry	9
(d) RTO employees have salaries set according to market value for similar positions in industry	5
(e) RTO employees have salary guidelines that are set according to market position while the actual salary is set based on the employee's performance against targets	8
(f) Same as (e), although the money provided to the employees is partly salary and partly bonus	6
(g) RTO has situation (b), and has developed a mechanism to enable it to provide the employees additional money based on performance of the individual and the RTO	3

Observation on best practice: Setting salary ranges with market information and rewarding individual employees with base salary and bonuses based on performance, is the *best* practice. There is total agreement that a compensation package has to be competitive enough to be able to attract the best people. The same is not always possible in a typical government system. It appears that a trust under government patronage can overcome such problems.

8.5   Compensation package decision making

To decide on the compensation package for employees to reward their contribution to the RTO and to encourage high performance.

Project performance indicators

1. Assessment of process success
2. RTO performance

Practices	Number of RTOs
(a) The compensation package is provided by the owner or governing body and the RTO has no control over it	22
(b) The RTO chief decides on how much to pay each employee according to an informal process	4
(c) The RTO chief decides on how much to pay each employee according to a formal process	1
(d) The RTO managers decide alone on how much to pay their staff according to an informal process	1

(e) The RTO managers decide alone on how much to
    pay their staff according to a formal process   8
(f) The RTO managers decide together how much salary
    to pay their staff according to a formal process   4

Observation on best practice: The *best* practice is for all the managers to decide
together, on the salaries, for all the employees using a formal process. This has
the added benefit of helping the management form new teams to respond to new
opportunities, because they have learned the capabilities of every staff member
through the evaluation process. There is total agreement that a compensation
package has to be competitive enough to be able to attract the best people. The
same is not always possible in a typical government system. It appears that a trust
under government patronage can overcome such problems.

8.6   Non-pay based rewards

To encourage and reward high performance in ways other than salaries and
bonuses.

Project performance indicators

1. Assessment of rewards used
2. RTO performance

Practices	*Number of RTOs*
(a) No rewards are given	22
(b) Informal award sessions (i.e. cake and coffee party) for individuals who have done something significant	4
(c) Formal awards where individuals are recognized for significant contributions (citation)	12
(d) Formal awards where individuals are recognized for significant contributions and given a significant cash prize	3
(e) Granting of the right to attend certain international meetings as a reward for high performance	15
(f) A combination of awards and recognition events are used	8

Observation on best practice: Having a combination of awards and recognition
events is the *best* practice. In Asian RTOs except for the Japanese prefecture laboratories, there is no significant reward giving system other than promotions
which means increments in salary and bonus. In the prefecture laboratories
of Japan, there is no formal promotion system but good performance by the
research team is recognized in the form of non-cash rewards like citation.

8.7   Staff evaluation

To identify the need for improvement in the staff performance, capability-
building, career planning and so on.

Project performance indicators

1. Assessment of RTO technical strength
2. Growth in client revenue
3. Client interaction

Practices	*Number of RTOs*
(a) Staff evaluation is not done	13
(b) Supervisor subjectively evaluates performance and verbally recommends improvements	9
(c) The RTO sets broad objectives for all, supervisor subjectively evaluates and formally (written) recommends improvements	3
(d) Supervisor sets employee specific objectives, evaluates against those objectives and formally informs of improvements needed	15
(e) The RTO sets broad objectives for all, supervisor participates with other managers in a comprehensive evaluation of all	2

Observation on best practice: Staff evaluation is generally a part of promotional policies and capability building activities (HRD) in all the RTOs studied. In every case, there are formal as well as informal procedures as outlined in practices for promotion, capability building and career planning, training, reward and so on. The *best* practice is to have the RTO set broad objectives and evaluation methods. Managers together evaluate all staff against the broad objectives on the basis of the objective evaluation methods.

8.8 Discharging staff

To have only the staff required to meet the RTO's needs by being able to remove staff that are not needed.

Project performance indicators

1. Assessment of satisfaction
2. RTO performance
3. Number of staff laid off or leaving voluntarily
4. Number of staff fired

Practices	*Number of RTOs*
(a) The RTO cannot remove unwanted staff because of legal or cultural requirements	24
(b) It is legally possible to remove unwanted staff but, because the process is so difficult, it is almost never done	10
(c) The RTO can remove staff due to insufficient revenue to support them (i.e. layoffs) without too much difficulty, but has great difficulty removing staff for other reasons	10
(d) The RTO has authority to discharge staff and, as long as the proper procedures are followed (documentation of unsatisfactory performance and attempts to improve performance), does discharge staff that do not meet the needs of the RTO	9
(e) The RTO can and does discharge staff with little effort	5

Observation on best practice: In fact, although it is legally possible to discharge staff, the social and economic systems do not make it possible to do so. The legal procedure is also so complex and time consuming that most of the RTOs studied avoid the legal courses available to them. Having the authority to discharge staff can be considered as a good practice for the RTO so that the non-performers can be discharged. It is not practised in most of the RTOs except for five RTOs out of the 60 that we have covered in our study.

8.9 Internal communication

To instill an understanding of common purpose in the employees and an appreciation of other's roles in that purpose.

Project performance indicators

1. Assessment of methods used
2. RTO size
3. RTO performance

Practices	*Number of RTOs*
(a) The RTO does not have formal internal communication systems although communication flows well because the RTO is small	21
(b) The RTO does not have formal internal communication systems even though the RTO is large (1–5 methods of communication)	17
(c) The RTO makes a reasonable effort at communication (6–10 methods of communication)	17
(d) The RTO makes a reasonable effort to communicate with and among staff (>10 methods of communication)	3

Observation on best practice: All practices are good practices. The best practice has to be a combination of all. In general the RTOs also felt that regular staff meetings with technical advisory or similar committees is of great help.

9 Networking

Sub-Processes

1. Networking with technology providers
2. Networking with industry to better understand needs

9.1 Networking with technology providers

To develop mutually beneficial relationships with other technology providers.

Project performance indicators

1. Assessment of process used
2. Growth in client revenue
3. RTO financial performance
4. Networking table results

Practices	*Number of RTOs*
(a) The RTO places little emphasis on encouraging networking	13

(b) The RTO encourages networking and pays for several
     lower-cost activities   23
(c) The RTO strongly encourages networking and pays for
     several low-cost and some higher-cost activities,
     more effective methods   24

Observation on best practice: The developing countries' RTOs cannot afford to pay for wide networking. The *best* practice is to support some low-cost and some high-quality networking activities.

9.2 Networking with industry to better understand needs

To develop mutually beneficial relationships with industries that the RTO is serving.

Project performance indicators

1. Growth in client revenue
2. Client interactions

Practices	*Number of RTOs*
(a) Industry actively serves on the RTO board	19
(b) Industry is on advisory committees that help plan RTO work	16
(c) RTO technical staff attend meetings and functions where industry is present	15
(d) RTO technical staff serves on industry committees	19
(e) The RTO trains students bound for industry resulting in people that know the RTO working in industry	4
(f) The RTO holds seminars for industry	34
(g) The RTO forms a club that the industry joins and gets subsidized services	2

Observation on best practice: Best practice is a combination of practices from (a) to (g). The basic purpose is to enhance the process of linkage between the RTO and the firms/industry.

10 Policy and programmes

Sub-Processes

1. The role of the RTO in science and technology and industrial development policies
2. Use of government programmes

10.1 The role of the RTO in science and technology and industrial development policies

To help the country (or other political units, like provinces) form its science and technology and industrial development policies.

Project performance indicators

1. Assessment of RTO's role

Practices	*Number of RTOs*
(a) The RTO plays no role	15
(b) The RTO as an organization advises the government on elements of science and technology	4
(c) The RTO is charged with the formal development of science and technology policy	1

Observation on best practice: The best practice would be to have the RTO experts on various government panels so that they get an opportunity to advice the government on certain science and technology policy issues.

10.2 Use of government programme

To take advantage of government programmes that help the RTO to meet its goals.

Project performance indicators

1. RTO financial performance
2. Growth in RTO (budget or size)
3. Assessment of RTO's use of programmes
4. Percentage of budget from government contracts

Note:

This process is generally beyond the RTO's control in that if there are no programmes to access, the RTO cannot access them. However, including this as a sub-process demonstrates the role that government programmes can play in the success of RTOs. In environments where there are no programmes, the RTO will have more difficulty meeting financial goals without government grant support.

Practices	*Number of RTOs*
(a) No programmes are available that can help the RTO	5
(b) The RTO helps clients apply for programmes that support R&D by making them aware of the programme and by writing proposals in a fashion that helps the client get funding to pay for work at the RTO	8
(c) The RTO provides free services to clients as part of a contract with the government programme that wants the services to be provided	12
(d) The RTO provides subsidized services to clients as part of a contract with the government programme that wants the service to be provided	13
(e) The RTO uses national and international programmes to fund internal capability improvements	10
(f) The RTO acquires funding by responding to government programme request for proposals for R&D in certain technologies	12
(g) The RTO uses government programmes to lever industry money	7

Observation on best practice: It is suggested that using government programmes to fund internal capability improvements is the best practice.

Index